ANALYSIS OF THE PROBLEM OF WAR

By

CLYDE EAGLETON

PROFESSOR OF GOVERNMENT, NEW YORK UNIVERSITY

THE RONALD PRESS COMPANY

NEW YORK

PRINTED IN THE UNITED STATES OF AMERICA

PREFACE

Recently, the danger of being pulled into a war has aroused a frantic interest in our foreign policy. American thinking concerning international affairs has of course been disoriented during the past decade or so; before that, little attention had been given to international problems. Various theories have been offered to explain our entry into the World War, each claiming to be sufficient in itself, and each the proper basis for a solution of the problem of war. Many of these ideas are hasty and thoughtless; some of them are fantastic. The political situation arising from the effort to legislate us out of war has heightened the confusion.

War, of course, is no simple problem, and the effort to uproot it leads into many ramifications. It does seem possible, however, to seek out some fundamental principles by which to guide one's thinking, and to test the various schemes before us by these. The American people now have a real interest in the problem; and the dangers revealed in some of the current proposals, as well as their inconsistency with American traditions and principles, have disposed them to make a serious study of the problem.

There have been many organizations working, each in its own way, for peace, with a resultant confusion in the movement for peace which is shocking. The organization of the National Peace Conference, including over thirty of the leading national organizations working for peace in the United States, gives hope for improvement in this situation. The purposes of these groups vary, but they have been able to reach a common platform of agreement. It is my firm belief that a much greater degree of agreement can be reached when the American people have thought the problem through. I am encouraged to believe this because of certain fundamental principles of American political and moral philosophy, now innate in American character, which furnish the answer to many questions before us today, if only one takes the trouble to bring them into focus. When one has seen why peoples are unwilling to surrender the right to make war and what would be the consequences of such a surrender, it is easier to attack the problem.

This is my reason for adding another to the long list of books dealing with war. Its purpose is to establish some fundamentals and to test against them the chief proposals now under consideration for the control of war. It is presented in as brief and simple form as possible in the hope that it will not be too burdensome to read and that it may provoke some thought toward the solution of the most vital problem facing the community of nations.

CLYDE EAGLETON

CONTENTS

ANALYSIS OF THE PROBLEM OF WAR

CHAPTER I

THE PROBLEM OF WAR

If everyone is opposed to war, why do we have war?

It is only the slightest of exaggeration to say that everyone is opposed to war. There may be an occasional Goering, or Mussolini, to boast of the inherent virtues of war; even they, it may be suspected, have ulterior motives, and do not consider war itself as desirable or virtuous. There are many who, while hating war, feel nevertheless that its use upon occasion is justifiable. But persons who approve of war as a desirable institution are rarely to be found. Why, then, do we have war?

It is a vexing question, which leaves many a person impatient, and inclined to put the blame upon human depravity. Original sin, however, is not the answer, for war is simply a method, a weapon, which may be used for a good purpose or for a bad purpose, but which is not an end in itself. Like a sword or a gun, it cannot itself be described as sinful; the sin is to be found in the person who uses it, or in the motives for which it is used. One's thinking, then, must go beyond the mere question of eliminating war; no final answer is to be found there.

Few people realize this fact. Most are content to hate war itself, and they apparently expect the curse to disappear simply because they hate it. If it were this simple, war would have disappeared long ago. But war is an ancient and well-established institution, with its roots deeply fixed in the past. For centuries it has been accepted and glorified; it is connected in our thoughts with such terms, glorious in their connotation, as honor, and defense, and patriotism, and the maintenance of rights. It is no simple evening chore to uproot so traditional an institution; it is not to be eradicated by wishful thinking, or by a treaty, or by a number of treaties in a row. And so far, we have had little but wishful thinking. Sunday sermons and Armistice Day speeches are full of beautiful quotations from the Bible and from the poets; newspapers and pamphlets horrify us with ghoulish pictures of the increasing brutality of war. All this is a work of supererogation, for no one needs to be convinced that war is brutal, or that peace is desirable. The question is not: Do we wish to get rid of war? That one is answered. The question which now faces us is: How *can* we get rid of war? This is a question for experts—for statesmen and international lawyers; but the answers which they find must be submitted to their peoples, and the peoples must decide for or against them in accordance with fundamental human feelings, with accepted moral principles, and with their own ideas as to material self-interest.

It is time for the preacher and the orator to suspend their fulminations and to pass on to the next stage. They—and others—must start their thinking from the point to which we have now won, that there is a universal desire to abandon war. The work of constructive building must be undertaken; and here the old difficulty presents itself. So long as the campaign is one of attack, of destruction, agreement is easy; but when the work of construction begins, the architects fall out among themselves. Already there are innumerable panaceas offered by those who have advanced thus far in their thinking.

It is probably true that there have been more words spoken and written and wasted in the cause of peace than for any other human ideal; and still we have war with us. It is all very confusing and very sad; it should at least teach us that we have no easy problem. What are we driving at? To abolish war, certainly; but how? Is it possible to discover some fundamentals in this problem, and thus to lay a foundation upon which to build? It is usually correct to lay the foundation first; but few of those who offer us panaceas have taken the trouble to lay a foundation for their building. They have, for the most part, regarded war as an evil spirit, to be exorcised by loud incantations. It is much more of a problem than this. War continues because it has its uses; and herein lies the problem.

We have not been able to get rid of war because we have provided nothing to put into its place. War is a method of achieving purposes; it must be replaced with other and satisfactory methods for achieving these purposes before it will be dropped from use. Doubtless, many of the purposes for which war has been used should never be permitted to be achieved; but, incredible as it may sound to one who hates war, it is nevertheless a fact that war is used to serve certain necessary functions. For centuries, war has been regarded as a means of remedying unjust situations, of settling disputes, of enforcing rights. That human ingenuity could hardly have devised a more stupid and inefficient method of performing these functions does not alter the situation; no other method has been provided by statesmen or peoples for the discharge of these duties.

It must be conceded that these are essential functions in any human society. The first duty of government is to maintain peace and order between its members; this is the *raison d'être* of the state. In any human society which hopes to avoid violence and to assure the undisturbed development of its individual members, means must be provided for the settlement of disputes, for the improvement of unfair conditions, and for the enforcement of the rights of its members. We have long been accustomed to the performance of these functions within the state by an authority to which all must submit; within the community of nations they are not so well provided for. The development of the latter community has of course been much slower; for long, it has had only the inadequate method of war to perform all these functions.

Under such a system, a dispute will ultimately be settled in favor of the stronger state. The weaker state will rarely be able to repair its injustices; only the more powerful state can enforce its rights. It means that might makes right, which is blasphemy in any system of ethics. But the fact remains that during all these centuries human beings have employed war for these purposes, and that not even yet have they provided machinery enough better to justify abandoning war.

It follows, with inescapable logic, that no state will be willing to surrender its right to make war until a substitute is found which, in the judgment of that state, will satisfactorily perform these vital functions. It would, indeed, be a betrayal of its very existence for a state to do so. Aristotle said—and he is still read with approval by political scientists—that the purpose of the state is to advance the well-being of its members. The state must, then, protect its national existence; and it must protect and promote the interests of its members. Why else should it exist? The long accepted method by which it seeks to achieve these ends is—ultimately—war; and that war is the worst possible means makes no difference in our problem, except in so far as it forces us to seek better means. No state will surrender the means which it now has for protecting and promoting the interests of its members until other means are offered in which it can have confidence.

The preceding paragraphs contain hard facts, not generally recognized. They may be made slightly more understandable, if not more palatable, by translating them into hypothetical situations. [Force used in self-defense is universally regarded as justified; and war constitutes this defensive force as between nations. But what is self-defense? A boundary dispute may arise in which the other nation seizes territory and citizens which you claim, and refuses any form of pacific settlement—a situation which not infrequently arises in the case of boundary disputes. It is not quite a case of self-defense, for the boundary is not legally established; would a war to maintain your claim be justifiable, there being no other way to obtain a settlement? To carry it a little further afield, suppose that the states which favor a dictatorial form of government—a dozen or more—should combine and set out to make a totalitarian world. When they had arrived to invade the United States, there would be little doubt as to the propriety of a war in defense against such an attack; but might it not be wise to go to war a little earlier, say, when England is under attack? For if England and other democracies were defeated, our own defense would be much more difficult. History, of course, has never recorded a war which was not a defensive war, and defensive on both sides.

The situation might easily be reversed. Perhaps you think an offensive war would be worth while to extend Fascism, or Communism, or Christianity, or anti-vivisection, or whatever weighs most upon your mind. It has taken quite a lot of force, some of it in the form of war, to eradicate slavery, there being no international governmental authority which could decree slavery illegal and enforce the decree against resistance. There have been wars in our own history which the people were willing to fight because of humanitarian motives; perhaps in these cases they were deluded, but they nevertheless thought war justifiable for such purposes.

Most of the states in the world today are founded upon revolution; most peoples would assert a right of revolution. If this use of force is justifiable, so is war; the same logic stands behind both. If internal oppression of rights justifies forceful resistance, external oppression of rights may likewise justify forceful action. If revolution may be justified against a despotic king, or against a privileged class, in order to obtain more individual freedom or better assurance of a livelihood, similarly the use of war may be approved against a Napoleon, enslaving peoples or sending them to death to serve his own selfish purposes, or to assure a people a share in the resources of nature unfairly held and selfishly used by others. If revolution is the ultimate recourse against an established situation, so may war be. War has been called the *ultima ratio regis;* it may also be the last recourse of a people. When a starving man steals, a jury may give him mercy, and the state will attempt to remedy the desperate situation in which he is caught up; but there is no such machinery of international government; thus far, there is only war.

It is difficult to persuade an American to think in terms of needs or rights outside his own boundaries, for the United States is so nearly self-sufficing that we could dispense with these needs or rights at no great material sacrifice. There would be many Americans, however, who would be inclined to ask questions, or even to take vigorous action, if deprived of their coffee for breakfast. A man can live without coffee, but why should he? If American industry were deprived of rubber, even more vigorous questions would be asked. In a rapidly increasing degree, American citizens are coming to be affected in that most vital spot, the pocketbook, by what happens abroad. The grain raiser in the middle west, who reads the *Chicago Tribune,* and wishes to have nothing to do with foreign nations, is beginning to realize that the price which he receives for his wheat has long been fixed at Liverpool; the cattleman, who wonders why the shoes he buys cost more than the steer he sells, is probably ignorant of our long diplomatic controversy with the Argentine, or of the fact that the League of Nations has held an international conference on Hides and Bones; the insouciant little school teacher, who has invested her savings in Electric Bond and Share, is shocked to find that her proceeds may be affected by a revolution down in Brazil. When translated into the actual dependence of our inhabitants upon foreign countries, such matters as the maintenance of foreign trade and of fair markets and access to necessary materials cease to be a question of whether the Standard Oil Company, or other such corporation, is making money for itself, and become a question of vital concern to each individual.

They are also matters of vital concern to the community of nations. In such things as raw materials, or capital, or markets, there are mutual interests as between nations; and the community recognizes the need for protecting these interests by international law. To say that a man who invests or works abroad does so for his own gain and deserves no protection, does not accurately represent the situation. Doubtless his purposes are purely selfish; but so are those of the butcher and the baker and the groceryman who set up their respective shops. The latter supply the needs of life in their respective communities; and, while they certainly do not act for altruistic purposes, the community gives them protection and support. Similarly, the citizen who goes abroad to sell shoes, or oil, or steel, or to buy bananas, or rubber, or whatnot, serves vital needs both of his nation and of the community of nations; and though his motives are selfish, he nevertheless deserves and is given the protection of international law. If the business in which he is engaged is of sufficient importance to his own state, that state may feel it necessary to support him—or rather, the interest which he represents—even to the point, in the absence of other means, of making war. War may be, and of course is, a poor means of protecting this interest; but until a better way is found, war will be used.

If the self-sufficing American could put himself into the position of the citizen of some other state, he could understand this situation better. As an Englishman, for example, he would realize that he would starve in a very few weeks if he were cut off from his sources of supply outside of England; indeed, responsible ministers in England have boasted of building up a store of food for three weeks ahead, as part of the recent rearmament program. Today, Japan and Italy are arguing that they must have more reliable sources of supply for their overflowing populations, and that in the absence of any community machinery for this purpose, they must resort to the use of force. Supposing that the truth of their claims were granted, what other recourse have they? Force has always been the final arbitrament where better means of adjustment do not prevail; and the absence of force within a community is in direct proportion to the presence of other means for the settlement of disputes, the remedying of injustice, and the enforcement of rights agreed upon in the community.

The above paragraphs may sound like a defense of war, but they are not so intended; their purpose is rather to show why war continues. The emphasis lies not upon the virtues of war but upon the need to provide better means than war for serving functions which are absolutely essential in any community. As between individuals within the state, such means have been provided, and are steadily being added to, as new needs arise. Yet even within the state these means have never been sufficient; not even the state, with all its centuries of development behind it, has been able to perform these functions in so satisfactory a fashion that force could be entirely excluded.

Much less, of course, has the community of nations been able to do it. Indeed, only within the past century have nations begun to think of the problem at all; only within the last decade or so have they begun to provide agencies for the purpose; indeed, it is only within the last year or so that they have realized the need of a means for altering a *status quo* or remedying an unjust situation against the wishes of those in possession. But the same forces are now at work in the community of nations as caused the remarkable extension of government between individuals; that is to say, the forces of interdependence. At the time when the Constitution of the United States was made, individuals were so self-sufficing that Thomas Jefferson could say: "that government is best which governs least." It is no longer possible to take such a position. Times have changed so that citizens now demand governmental interference. How, but for such governmental action, could you be sure that the hands which prepared your food, in a far-away canning factory, or even in the restaurant in which you sit, were not filthy with disease? How can the natural resources upon which the nation depends be preserved against reckless misuse by individual owners, except by governmental control? The interdependence between individuals, growth of the last century, has necessitated the creation of governmental agencies and laws in ever increasing measure, to protect the individual against his fellow upon whom he depends.

The same interdependence is now at work between nations. As it increases, more causes of conflict arise, and peoples are faced with the alternative from which law is born: eternal fighting, or submission to a community rule. It is that pressure which is today pushing nations into closer cooperation through the making of new international law and the creation of new international machinery.

The situation may be looked at from another viewpoint. The most fundamental problem of government, wherever found, has always been the extent to which government should interfere with individual liberty. Men have always struggled to preserve as much of their liberty as possible; similarly, nations struggle to preserve as much of their sovereignty as possible. For some time, individuals asked no more of government than to protect life and property; today, in the intricacy of modern life, they demand more. It is the good old paradox: the more government we have, the more liberty we have. Only now does the community of nations begin to feel this pressure; only now is it beginning to learn that a war anywhere is injurious to all. The lesson elsewhere learned, in the long school of experience, that individual liberty must be restrained at the point where it interferes with the liberty of other individuals, has not yet been adopted between nations; but the demand for it increases steadily, and will necessarily continue to increase as long as national units continue to exist as members of a community having common interests. National sovereignty must be restrained: this may be done as in the past by individual action, or it may be by the combined force of all; but it will assuredly be restrained, by one or the other method, where invasion of the rights of others cannot otherwise be prevented.

It is against the background above described that the problem of war must be viewed. Human beings demand, and should demand, certain rights. What these rights are, and how they should be protected, may be a matter of dispute; but unless other and satisfactory agencies are provided for the purpose, human beings may decide for themselves what their rights are, and will endeavor to protect those rights by their own might. And the same human beings, organized into states—which, after all, are merely agencies for furthering the well-being of the individual—will use force, or war, to protect and further their group rights and interests.

It is important to remember that war, or the elimination of war, is not an end in itself. War, it must be repeated, is simply a method, a weapon, which may be used for worthy or for unworthy purposes. War is one of the various forms in which violence manifests itself; consequently, we cannot limit our study to war alone, but must reach out into the broader field in which physical force is exercised. Our problem is not so much how we shall get rid of war, as how we shall be able to control and direct the use of force for desirable ends. Like fire, in the physical world, force, in the political realm, may be either destructive or constructive. Uncontrolled, fire is one of the most dreaded of the evils which may befall the human race; it is listed with war itself, and with plague and earthquake and flood, as a fearful destructive force. Yet it is at the same time, when properly directed, utterly indispensable in life. Locked up within the fireproof walls of a furnace, protected by gauges and thermostats and other scientific devices, its energy thus directed into proper channels, fire runs the machinery of industry, provides us with the means of communication, cooks our meals and heats our homes. But fire has not always been so safe or so useful; human ingenuity has tamed it for human uses. Even now, it breaks forth with destructive activity at times, and compels men to fight for their lives against it.

Human ingenuity must be utilized in the same manner to harness the destructive energies of violence and to direct them into useful channels. Within the state this has been done, though it is no more to be hoped than in the case of fire that an absolute control can be attained, and that no harm whatsoever shall be suffered from its use. Perhaps science will some day provide us with atomic energy, or other thing, to replace fire; then we may lay fire aside, and never have to risk its dangers again. Perhaps political science will some day supply us with a better means of maintaining law and order than through the use of physical force, in which case violence will no longer be needed by governments. But until these happy discoveries are made, we must continue to use fire and we must continue to use force. Our task is to control and direct their energy into useful channels; would that statesmen had been as successful as scientists in this effort!

The chief difficulty in the peace movement today is the

oversimplification of peace in the average mind, and even in the intelligent mind. Some would say that war is vicious, and that they will never again support war; some feel that war is simply another European villainy, and that we may avoid war simply by remaining neutral; supporters of the outlawry of war movement have achieved their end when they say, in the Pact of Paris, *fiat pax!* The average person is inclined simply to shrug war away, saying "I will have nothing to do with such brutal conduct"; which is much like saying: "I shall have nothing to do with the next economic depression, because I do not like depressions."

Unfortunately, we cannot be rid of war by hating it, or disdaining it, or ostracizing it. It must seem a little strange even to ardent haters of war, that human beings should have for so long permitted the scourge of war to continue, for no reason whatsoever. Surely war has not been regarded as a pleasure, and maintained for that purpose! Not all wars have been fought for sadistic enjoyment; not all statesmen who have ordered war, or legislators who have voted for wars, were in league with the devil. In most cases, they, and their peoples behind them, went to war soberly and hesitantly, or perhaps too angrily and hastily, but in either case, convinced that it was a necessary step for the protection of interests or the maintenance of rights. Perhaps they were mistaken as to their rights; perhaps they were mistaken in the use of war as a method for protecting those rights; nevertheless, they had an end in view, and they employed war because there was no other machinery available to gain that end. It is without question true that war has often been used for unjust purposes; and it is to be doubted in many cases whether the use of war accomplished any improvement in the situation—though it does seem somewhat of an exaggeration to say that war never settled a dispute and never righted a wrong. But, leaving this point to the historians, the fact remains that nations have thought that there were some things worth fighting for, if they could not be otherwise achieved; and that they knew of no other means than war for obtaining them. And this continues to be a fact.

Peace, we are now realizing, is no mere negative status. It is not the mere absence of war, as cold is the absence of heat. We are not seeking a frozen *status quo*. War is not an end in itself; no more is peace an end. There are some things more to be desired than peace; and if they cannot be achieved in peace, they will be sought in war. Peace may mean no more than surrender to a criminal; it can mean a situation of degradation and suffering more hateful than war itself. Men have always, and should always, seek progress; so civilization has been builded. Peace must have machinery to provide for this progress; if the machinery is not provided, there will be no peace. War and revolution have been necessary in the past to remove obstructions from the path of progress; it is a bitter comment upon human intelligence that this should be true. It is possible to have progress without war, but this presupposes a satisfactory substitute for war. It means much new building, doubtless at much cost to established convictions, and perhaps even at the cost of some blood. It means that physical force must be forbidden to separate states, as it has been forbidden to individuals within the state; and to secure this, it may be necessary to employ overwhelming physical force against the state which wrongfully uses violence. We must provide also means for redressing wrongs, and caring for needs, and enforcing rights, before nations will be willing to surrender the means they have so long employed—war. It is a long and laborious task, upon which we are just entering.

The time is past, then, for vain maledictions and evocations against war; it is time for profound study of the substitutes which international society must provide in place of war. We propose now to test the various proposals currently under discussion for the elimination of war against the background above given. The question to be asked concerning each of them is: How far does this proposed method of controlling or eliminating war offer a satisfactory substitute for war as a means of settling disputes, of remedying wrongs, and of enforcing rights?

CHAPTER II

DISARMAMENT

In disarmament the United States has put most of its faith and hope, if not quite so much of charity. Along with the Pact of Paris, embodying the slogan "outlaw war," it has been the contribution of the United States toward the cause of peace in the world. And not merely the United States, but all nations have joined in an exhaustive study and in an effort almost desperate at times, to secure an agreement for the reduction of armaments. The effort, it may now be said without fear of contradiction, has failed completely, and this for the simple reason that it attempted to put the cart before the horse. The effort has been to eliminate war by eliminating armaments; the logical and necessary procedure is to get rid of war, after which there will be no need for armaments. So long as peoples continue to regard war as a necessary weapon, no state will give up its right to make war; and so long as a state claims the right to make war, it will certainly not, and logically it should not, be ready to surrender or reduce its arms.

This is reasonable enough; it is also proven by experience. The First Hague Conference was called to reduce the "staggering burden of armament"; instead, it promulgated a Convention for the Pacific Settlement of International Disputes, and builded the Permanent Court of Arbitration at the Hague. When the Second Hague Conference was being prepared, there was much dispute as to whether disarmament should be put upon the agenda at all, and it was finally dropped therefrom; this Conference, also, addressed itself to the method by which disputes were to be settled.

Among the famous Fourteen Points of President Wilson, which were to serve as the basis for peace in the World War, was one which demanded that national armaments should be "reduced to the lowest point consistent with national safety." When this was debated at the Peace Conference, France was more interested in protecting herself against German attack in the future than in weakening her own military strength. It was a logical position, and was so recognized by President Wilson when he accepted the ill-fated proposal for a treaty of guarantee. His idea was finally incorporated into the Covenant of the League of Nations, but as a reduction of armaments rather than as disarmament. Total disarmament is in fact a will o' the wisp, until total security is provided from the outside—a sort of a political problem in the infinitesimal theory. It has also its practical difficulties. When Litvinov proposed total disarmament, he was twitted with the fact that Russia has the longest frontier and the largest area of any state in Europe; consequently, the police necessary for its protection would constitute a larger army than any other state would have, after military establishments had been abandoned.

The effort, then, has been restricted to the limitation and reduction of armaments. This was the principle adopted in the Covenant of the League; and the acceptance of this principle was in fact an acknowledgment that disarmament was a hopeless endeavor, and that the best which could be hoped for was a saving in cost. Article 8 of the Covenant stated, on the one hand, national safety and, on the other hand, sufficient force to enforce international obligations, as the criteria for reduction; and so long as national safety remains as uncertain as it now is, states need not be expected to reduce their armaments with much enthusiasm. The Covenant fixes no obligation in this respect; it merely states a *desideratum.*

It is true, however, that the League of Nations has worked sincerely and vigorously to achieve this objective. It has held innumerable meetings, of all sorts; the study which it has made has been both exhaustive and exhausting. It is hardly possible that a more sincere and thorough effort could have been made than has been carried out under the auspices of the League; and in this work the United States has actively participated. Yet the whole history of the endeavor can be summed up in the change of title of a committee: the League started with a Commission on the Reduction of Armaments, and it ended with a Committee on Arbitration, Security, and Disarmament. The order of words is significant; it represents the evolution of the thinking of the League.

The earliest effort of the League was a direct effort to reduce arms, but it soon became evident that other factors must be taken into consideration. In 1922, Lord Robert Cecil offered a resolution, accepted by the Assembly, which laid down the principle that "in the present state of the world, many governments would be unable to accept the responsibility for a serious reduction of armaments unless they receive in exchange a satisfactory guarantee of the safety of their country." In accordance with this orientation, an effort was made to adopt a Treaty of Mutual Assistance, and following that, the Geneva Protocol, which marks the greatest advance yet made by the community of nations toward the control of war. It failed to secure ratification, largely because Great Britain was uncertain whether the United States would maintain its rights as a neutral in case of a League blockade against a Covenant-breaking state. Blocked in the effort to provide the necessary security of states, the disarmament movement again turned to direct methods; but the Disarmament Conference which met in 1933, in spite of the prodigious work of its Preparatory Commission and the indefatigable labors of its President, Arthur Henderson, proved utterly futile. Disarmament is concededly a dead issue now, though obligations arising from the past must still be given formal observance.

The divergent methods above suggested are described by Señor de Madariaga in what yet remains the best book on the subject of disarmament, as the direct and the indirect method. The official attitude of the United States, apparently supported by public opinion, has been the direct method. It derives from the assumption that arms and preparedness lead to war; it follows, therefore, that if we could get rid of arms, we should also be rid of war. The argument can be valid only if there are no other causes of war, which is obviously not true. If armaments are a cause of war, there are also many other causes of war; and if armaments should be removed, these causes would still be operative. There would still be disputes, and resort to violence; if there were no arms, men could still, and would still, fight with their fists and with sticks and stones. Doubtless the loss and suffering would not be so great—which is certainly to be desired—but the fundamental problem—war itself—would remain. Armaments, like war itself, serve simply as an instrument, a means toward some end; if armaments were abolished, war, or force, would still be employed for the furtherance of national policies. Yet the United States has clung consistently to this approach, throughout all discussions. She was unprepared to admit the other viewpoint—security—even to the extent of a willingness to consult when danger of war appeared. The Washington Arms Conference of 1922 is the only case of success in the effort at direct reduction of arms; and its gains were so trivial, and the animosities aroused by it were so great, that its effect upon the whole problem has been no more than that of a drop of water falling into a pool.

The League of Nations at first followed this method, with no success whatever. Following the resolution of Lord Robert Cecil, the League, as we noticed above, turned to the indirect method. Here the argument is reversed. Instead of saying that arms cause war, it is said that war causes arms. If this be true, then the attack must be upon war, rather than upon arms; and to the measure that fear of war is removed, in that measure will states be willing to reduce their armaments. In other, and familiar, words, there must be security before there can be disarmament. This was the motive which inspired the League of Nations to attempt the Treaty of Mutual Assistance and the Geneva Protocol, both still-born, and which finally eventuated in the limited regional guarantees of the Pact of Locarno. The return to the direct method, and its complete failure in the Disarmament Conference, underlines still further the necessity for providing security first.

Now, it is not to be denied that reduction of armaments is an end worthy in itself, though of comparatively minor importance. It is shocking to think that 75% to 90% of the national budget of the United States is wasted in the destructive costs of war, largely for armaments. To the average mind, the figures of these costs are incomprehensible; they are more comprehensible if stated in terms of comparison. Thus President Hoover remarked that our whole internal waterways system could be modernized for half the cost of a modern battleship. It has been estimated that the cost to the United States of two hours fighting in the World War would equal the entire budget of the League of Nations for one year; or, as Madariaga puts it, the total "defense budgets" of the world would meet the present expenses of the League of Nations, including the Court and the International Labor Organization, for six centuries. Such figures are incredible. When one thinks of the constructive work, the advance to human happiness, which could be achieved with these sums of money, one feels outraged. Mrs. Florence Boeckel, in her little book, *The Turn Toward Peace,* says: "One week of the World War cost the United States enough to build in every state 940 high schools at $100,000; 1,540 grade schools at $40,000; 480 churches at $100,000; and 1,920 recreation centres, with swimming pools and playgrounds, at $35,000. One half-year cost the United States enough to cover the purchase of one automobile and one tractor for every one of six and a half million farmers, with six hundred millions left over for good roads."

Nor is this cost to be measured in money alone. The finest characteristics of the human race are diverted to destructive purposes; the finest materials are sacrificed in war. Bitter complaints are raised when, in times of peace, millions of dollars are spent for relief, to save human lives; but the extravagant prices of war, paid to destroy human lives, are regarded as well justified. The extent to which human virtues can be distorted by such considerations has been recently revealed in the disclosures made in the munitions investigations. The losses in human character, and in economic ethics and methods, are as great as those which are measured in terms of money.

Such considerations deserve emphasis, for they help thinking people to realize how much more could be done for humanity if the destructive effects of war could be eliminated. Every possible reduction in the expenditures upon armaments is eagerly to be sought for; every dollar saved can be put to productive use. Reduction of armaments aids also to build a psychology of confidence between states, when it can be done; unfortunately, this confidence must be established before there can be much in the way of reducing armaments. These things are worth struggling for, even though there be little hope of large gains; the reduction of taxes may be regarded as an end in itself. It nevertheless remains true that there is little hope of accomplishment in this direction, and that even granted some reductions, it would contribute nothing to the actual solution of the problem of war.

We have looked at the logical difficulties of the disarmament approach; let us glance at the technical difficulties involved. They would fill pages; they do fill volumes of League of Nations documents. What, for example, is to be included in the term "armaments"? If we are to limit them, we should know what to limit. But a modern war makes use of practically all materials. A gun mounted on wheels is surely an implement of war; must we, then, limit the manufacture of wheels, and of axle-grease? Mules were used by the Italians in Ethiopia; must we therefore limit the production of mules? Airplanes have become important in peaceful commerce; must we stop building them because they can be loaded with bombs in time of war? Cotton, oil, chemicals, automobiles, and innumerable other things are indispensable to belligerents—indeed, if we attempt to limit the production of modern war materials, practically all industries would be put out of business.

Or again, who is to be counted in reducing the number of the military personnel maintained at such tremendous cost? Here is a rifle club, whose members employ their spare time in learning to shoot straight; and a *turnverein,* or athletic organization, whose members learn the coordinated movements which characterize military discipline—must they be forbidden? Even the Boy Scouts, and similar organizations, have been the subject of serious discussions at disarmament meetings. Much more serious would be the discussion of ordinary police and militia for the purpose of maintaining domestic order.

And again, what are the criteria by which the strength of one country is to be measured against that of another? Economic and industrial and geographic and other factors must be taken into consideration; modern wars are not won by men with guns alone. Even worse, what are the criteria by which the relative needs of states are to be determined? Great Britain asserts that for her far-flung possessions she must have the greatest navy in the world; can this be conceded by other states, when it means that they are at the mercy of this great navy, for whatever purpose it may happen to be used? Japan demands "parity," and what does this mean? It is suggested that military strength should be permissible only for purposes of defense; statesmen and research men must then define "aggression" and "self-defense"—thus far, they have not been successful. And who is to see to it that armaments, once limited, are maintained in their proper proportions? For it does seem that if nations could be trusted to respect their obligations, no arms would be needed by any state! And finally, if the purpose of war, and therefore of armaments, is to achieve national destiny or to accomplish national purposes, is it not the duty of every nation to build up its military strength to the highest possible degree?

Such questions make even a layman's head swim; they help to explain why the experts who have studied the question have made no better progress than they have. But, difficult as they are, they furnish no such insuperable obstacles to disarmament as does the desire for security. No people, and no statesman whose job depends upon his people, desires the terrible expenditure upon armaments. His surest way to popularity is to reduce the burden of taxation. But he submits to these expenses, and his people demand that he do so, because both he and his people feel that war, and the instruments of war, are still necessary in the anarchic organization of international society today. To believe that the statesman, or the average citizen who votes for him, has unjustifiable nationalistic or imperialistic ambitions, is, even when true, an inadequate explanation of the situation. In a world in which generosity or even respect for the rights of others does not always prevail, one may well hesitate, in the absence of a policeman, to throw away the instruments of self-protection.

Disarmament contributes nothing toward the necessary criteria established in the first chapter. It provides no pacific means for the settlement of international disputes; it merely makes it impossible to maintain your own end of the dispute when the other fellow is unwilling to listen to reason. It aids in no way to remedy an unfair situation; on the contrary, it deprives a people, in the absence of sufficient agencies of international government, of the only method of securing a remedy. And certainly it does nothing toward enforcing law and rights—a procedure which still seems to be necessary in this imperfect world, whether as between states or as between individuals.

Yet these are functions which must be served. No matter how poorly war may serve these ends, it is the accepted method, and the only method at present. There might be better methods, but they are not offered in the proposal for disarmament. Few persons, granted a proper understanding of the results, would be willing to make so complete a surrender of rights and hopes. For, unless these rights and hopes are protected by other means, the surrender of the means of making war puts the state which does so at the mercy of the state which is able to make war. Reduction in armaments, provided there is a corresponding reduction on the part of other nations, might reduce the amount of money spent and of blood shed, but it would not remove war, nor would it establish law and justice. And why should a state be willing to make reductions? If war is the means by which its people are to have their rights protected, or by which they are to achieve their ends, then it is the duty of each state to build its war-making power to the greatest strength possible. To what other logical result can the situation lead? Of course, this means that the state with the greatest military strength is the only one which can feel sure of protecting its rights or achieving its ends. It means, too, that reductions, so long as they are proportionate, will preserve the same relationship between states—unless, in the process of reduction, one state can trick another. Thus might makes right, which is a situation not to be endured; but disarmament does nothing whatever to improve the situation, further than a possible lessening of the cost.

On the other hand, if there were no need for war, there would be no need for arms. Governments would joyously discard their armaments and reduce their budgets, if they and their peoples could feel assured that protection and justice would be assured to them in some other way. Executives harassed by budget criticisms and the clamor for lower taxes are not eager to court unpopularity by increasing taxation; but they also face criticism if they do not prepare for the protection of the interests of these same people. They can be rescued from their dilemma only if protection is provided in some other manner. If a satisfactory substitute for war can be found, the problem of arms is automatically solved; and it can be solved in no other way.

CHAPTER III

MUNITIONS

Closely allied to the question of disarmament is that of the private trade in arms. The latter is, in fact, part of the former; but it has been forced out of its proper proportions through recent sensational books and through the publicity given to the recent investigations of the munitions industry. It is not a new question; international efforts to control the trade in arms reach back as far as 1890, when an organization for that purpose was established at Brussels. Current discussions have magnified its importance to such an extent as to divert attention from the main issue and to start many persons upon the wrong track in their thinking concerning the control of war.

The arms traffic is, of course, scandalous in many ways, and no brief in its behalf is intended here. From the viewpoint of this study, however, it is almost an irrelevant matter; it has little or nothing to do with the problem of eliminating the institution of war. The munitions industry does not produce war; rather, it results from war. If, on rare occasions—no one of which has been clearly established—it has actually produced a war (it needs no more for its purposes than a threat or fear of war), this is due to the fact that war as an institution exists. Were there no war, there would be no sale of munitions; but the proposition cannot be turned round to say: were there no munitions, there would be no war. Trade in arms is a mere parasite on the great beast of war; it feeds upon war, but it does not destroy war; nor would the destruction of the parasite destroy the beast. Its relation to the problem of removing war is the same as that of disarmament.

The scandals of the munitions industry need not be retold here. They were summed up in moderate but effective words by the Temporary Mixed Commission of the League of Nations in 1921:

"In general, the objections that are raised to untrammeled private manufacture may be grouped under the following headings:

1. That armament firms have been active in fomenting war scares and in persuading their own countries to adopt warlike policies and to increase their armaments.
2. That armament firms have attempted to bribe Government officials, both at home and abroad.
3. That armament firms have disseminated false reports concerning the military and naval programmes of various countries, in order to stimulate armament expenditures.
4. That armament firms have sought to influence public opinion through the control of newspapers in their own and foreign countries.
5. That armament firms have organized international armament rings through which the armament race had been accentuated by playing off one country against another.
6. That armament firms have organized international armament trusts which have increased the price of armaments sold to Governments."

According to an article in *Fortune,* it costs $25,000 to kill a man in modern warfare; for every man killed, then, $25,000 goes into the pockets of munitions makers. This is doubtless an overstatement, for some of it goes into other pockets; but even if it be lacking in mathematical exactitude, there is enough truth in it to arouse a sense of shock. This feeling, naturally perhaps, but not logically, is directed against munitions manufacturers; but it is war which puts the arms to use, and war which does the killing. If there were no private manufacturers of arms, these arms would still have to be made, so long as people regard war as essential. One may sympathize, and even agree, with those persons who assert that they would not care to make profits from such a business; yet, if everybody should refuse to aid in the manufacture of munitions necessary for national war, it might become necessary for the state to conscript persons to perform this service.

Logically — and ironically — the munitions manufacturer should, in the present situation, be regarded as a patriot deserving of the highest reward from his state. As things now stand, a nation may upon occasion desire to avail itself of the method by which intelligent man settles his disputes or maintains his national rights—which is to say, by killing as many as possible of his opponents in the dispute. So long as states employ war to attain their necessary or desired purposes, so long will they require arms; the man who provides these arms is in fact serving what are now regarded as the highest interests of his nation. It is thoroughly inconsistent of those people who make use of war to accomplish their desires, to censure those persons who supply them with the means for making the war.

Such a statement may shock many who have become accustomed to accepting the recent efforts to reduce the problem of war to a problem of munitions; but there is no use in blinking the facts. Emotional reactions have done so much to distort the perspective of the average person that it is necessary to recall these inconsistencies. One finds, for example, the statement that our munitions firms "actually" sold munitions to both sides in the Chaco conflict between Bolivia and Paraguay. By the same token, a smokeshop should not sell cigars to both Republicans and Democrats! So long as war is legitimate, an American owes no loyalty to either side in the conflict; there are good reasons, as we shall see, why both sides should be permitted to buy. It is not the selling of arms, nor the fact that they are sold to both sides, which is to be condemned; it is the use of these arms which is horrible; and this is due to war, not to trade. It is charged that the munitions people maintain a lobby in Washington; but even pacifist organizations do this. And what of the Tariff League? How does Mr. Shearer compare with Mr. Grundy? If war is legitimate, then the arms trade is as legitimate as any other trade; and if lobbying is legitimate for other industries, it is legitimate for the munitions industry. The pot calling the kettle black is no solution for the problem of war. There are other industries—oil, cotton, motors, etc.—which are almost as important for war purposes as are munitions, and which now show themselves as eager to sell for war purposes as do the munitions people.

The charge that our munitions manufacturers are equipping our potential enemies with materials for use in war against us need not create shock; the same is true of those who sell abroad such things as cotton, or copper, or oil, or scrap iron. Indeed, we should have to suspend most of our foreign trade if we wished to make sure that nothing we sell could ever be employed against us. For modern war calls for many things other than munitions. Cotton helps in the manufacture of explosives, and copper and scrap iron can be made into munitions of war. Even lipsticks contain glycerine, from which high explosives can be made!

If the above sounds like a defense of the munitions makers, it is not so intended; its purpose is rather to bring our problem back into the proper focus. There is no doubt that they have resorted to super-salesman methods which are open to reproach; they cannot be praised for the practice of bribery in high figures. They lose any claim to patriotism when they reveal to foreign governments military secrets which may prove damaging to their own countries. Above all, when they seek through propaganda to stir up hostility and enmity between states, they have committed an unforgivable crime. The indignation of the people against them is well deserved, and the government should take severe measures against them. But, from the viewpoint of our investigation, this is a domestic question of corrupt practice within an industry, which should be regulated by domestic law. The money spent upon the Nye investigation was well spent, from a domestic viewpoint. Such regulation might even avert a war; but it would contribute little to the general problem of eliminating war as an institution. It is a worthwhile effort, but in another field of endeavor. From our viewpoint, it is not the munitions manufacturers who must be attacked: it is war itself, and no one should be led away from this objective by his indignation at abuses within this group.

I confess that, personally, I should not care to be a munitions maker; but I should have to admit, at the same time, that it is a weak prejudice, unsupported by logic. I do not care to aid in the slaughter of my fellow human beings, but such slaughter, when designated as war, is the means accepted and approved in the present order for maintaining national honor and rights and defense. Why, then, should I feel squeamish about it? If one upholds the right to make war—as the United States does, the Kellogg Pact to the contrary nothwithstanding—then one should logically be willing to help provide the means for carrying on war. And if I am too sentimental or chicken-hearted myself to do this work, I should at least be able to admire the courage and manhood of those who do, in this manner, contribute to the defense of the nation.

Nor is this mere satire; it derives inevitably from the present situation. If it is satire, it is directed against the war system which makes the activities of munitions manufacturers patriotic and praiseworthy; or, to go a little deeper, against those persons who, unwilling for one or another reason to take the steps necessary to abolish war, relieve their consciences by taking it out on the munitions makers. It is absurd to say, as Seldes has recently said, that "no reason for war remains except sudden profits for the fifty men who run the munitions racket"; there are innumerable causes for war, and among them the desire of the munitions makers for profits is one of the least.

Nor is it any contribution—except toward levity—to suggest that war can be stopped by requiring that they be put into the front ranks of battle. Presumably, the purpose of such action would be to discourage the manufacture of implements of war; but if there are reasons for not disarming, they are likewise reasons for continuing to make arms. It is the people—in democracies, at any rate—who make war; they furnish the munitions makers with an occupation.

It is not a sufficient answer to say that the people are misled by the propaganda of the munitions people. Of the existence of such propaganda there can unfortunately be no doubt; it has unquestionably fanned the flames of national hostility, and perhaps has assisted in the production of actual wars. This is probably the most serious charge which can be directed against munitions makers; there can be no defense for such viciously selfish action. It is in itself a matter to arouse violent indignation and strong measures should be taken against it; but it has little to do with the control of war. The munitions industry cannot be abolished until war is abolished; when this is done, all its evils will fall with it. No way has yet been found to control such propaganda; and there are innumerable other agencies whose propaganda leads toward war, whose inflammatory work would continue to stir up hostilities even after the munitions propaganda was stilled. Propaganda, like many other things, may be for a good or a bad cause; it is one of the problems of democracy that its voters must learn to distinguish between truth and falsehood. But this is a problem found in all other fields; it is not confined to the arms trade. Vicious as munitions propaganda is, equally vicious movements of propaganda can be found in newspapers and talks and literature in every field. That is another problem, the problem of democracy; it is not the problem of controlling war. At the most, it is simply one of many causes for war, and its elimination would not end war. And indeed, it would be impossible to eliminate it so long as war is regarded as proper and legitimate. Even to control it, or to restrain its worst features, is extremely difficult; to that we now turn our attention.

It is argued by some that the private manufacture of, or trade in, arms should be stopped, and that such work should be carried on by the government itself. This would not stop the manufacture of arms, nor lead to disarmament, nor eliminate war. It could only have the effect of removing some vices from one of many industries which need improvement in their methods, which is always to be desired; but it is no part of the problem of preventing war. It is simply a reform in business methods, to be put along with anti-trust laws, or public utility legislation, or the T.V.A.

And even so, it is not as simple a procedure as might be thought. There is nothing simple—as we have already seen—about disarmament; and control of the private manufacture and trade in arms is even more complicated. From the domestic viewpoint it raises grave questions which reach into the whole philosophy of government. To begin with, as Lehmann-Russbuldt pointed out in 1930, and as we learn from current neutrality discussions, the scope of war materials now embraces practically all the basic industries. Raw materials are the chief necessity in a modern war; this is the lesson which Italy learned. The bare suggestion that an embargo be laid upon oil led Mussolini to challenge the whole world. Between Japan and Italy even the scrap iron of this country has been cleaned out. No nation produces all that it needs in war; its requirements cover all fields of production. The result is that if a nation should really attempt to take the production of war materials out of private hands, it would have to nationalize practically all industries. This might not frighten some; but to many in the United States it would raise the red flag of socialism. It could not achieve its purposes if it permitted private manufacturers to supply belligerents with any of the potential materials of war; the competition among them would be as keen and as disgraceful as it now is among arms makers. This is a comparatively new situation, only slowly being recognized by the average citizen; evidence for it is already at hand in the attitude of shipping and oil and other industries toward Secretary Hull's efforts to stop their trade with Italy. It is easy to talk of taking over one industry, but one halts abruptly at the thought of taking over all the industries which are essential—almost as essential as arms—in the conduct of a modern war. It means nothing less than state socialism.

Here is a fundamental objection, at any rate in the United States; but this is only the beginning of the difficulties. If the government were to undertake to do its own manufacturing, it would, even if as efficient as could be desired, encounter grave obstacles. Its factories would be specialized, of use chiefly in time of war; they would be comparatively idle in peace time. To take up the slack suddenly when war breaks, to have the machines ready to go, to find skilled workers in sufficient numbers, would be almost impossible; inevitably, there would be a great waste in keeping the plants ready for the enormous expansion required by war. We are talking now of munitions plants alone; they could not be used, as private plants now are, for other industries in time of peace. If so, they would be overwhelmed by the complaints of business men that the government was competing with private industry by selling peace-time products, such as hunting equipment, or dynamite. Yet this would be necessary to prevent waste. Without it, there would be much unemployment, and the waste of vast idle equipment. Again, the government would practically be forced, through economic pressure, to enter into other fields; and again state socialism would be debated. Nationalization of such industries would doubtless aid in clipping off war propaganda—though even so, it could be used by governments, as it now is, for the purpose of securing increased appropriations. It might put an end to "war profits," to graft and bribery; as to this, governments have not always been able to escape corruption and extravagance, and even with efficiency, costs would be increased as above suggested.

From the international viewpoint, government manufacture produces even greater complications. Of the 70 odd states in the community of nations there are only some 20 which manufacture their own munitions of war; the manufacture of other materials of war, of course, varies enormously. The vast majority of states depend for their war supplies upon the private manufacturers within these 20 states; what would be their situation if the materials they need for war are manufactured by governments therein, instead of by private traders? This is the question which alarms them all. The great, consistent demand at League of Nations discussions on the part of non-producing states has been for an unrestricted right to buy munitions abroad. The Covenant itself, while agreeing that the "manufacture by private enterprise of munitions and implements of war is open to grave objections," instructs the Council to give due regard, in its efforts to remove these evil effects, "to the necessities of those Members of the League which are not able to manufacture the munitions and implements of war necessary for their safety."

A belligerent cannot, under the law of neutrality, buy arms from a neutral government, though it may buy from neutral individuals at their own risk. Consequently, if governments take over the manufacture of arms and control the trade therein, the majority of states would be unable to obtain arms in time of war; they would be forced either to purchase large quantities in time of peace —which would be wasted unless they should go to war— or else to undertake their own manufacture. If the latter course were followed, there would be far more munitions factories in the world, and probably far more munitions; in any case, the burden of armaments costs throughout the world would be enormously increased. And if the existence of munitions supplies—"preparedness"—leads to war, then the chances of war would be increased.

It is further true that if the small, or non-producing states must rely upon purchases from other governments (in peace time), they must have such purchases approved by the selling government; if they decide to build their own plants, they would probably have to borrow from such governments or from capitalists therein, and to seek technical experts and advice therefrom. In either case, the small countries would become dependent upon the large countries; and there would doubtless be a merry competition between the Great Powers to attach to themselves as many satellites, or allies, as possible through this dependency. Thus government control of arms would become an important factor in foreign policy, and the intrigues of diplomacy would become intensifiedly dangerous. So far as armaments go, the Great Powers would be little affected by a change to government control; it is they who are best equipped industrially, and who now produce the greatest amount of armaments. It is the small states which would suffer, both as to self-defense and as to independence in foreign policy. And what would become of the "right of revolution"?

The alternative to national manufacture and control is international control; but this seems so impracticable that little headway has been made in that direction. It is true that there have been international efforts, as far back as the Brussels Act of 1890. In this case, it was no more than to forbid trade in arms with certain parts of Africa. The attempt was to stop trade at its destination, which would be a more difficult task if there were destinations all over the world. The Convention of St. Germain, in 1919, proposed to limit exports, and to require reports on the trade from signatory states; but the United States refused to join, and of course other states would not accept obligations which would compel them to turn their markets over to the United States. International supervision was tried again in the Geneva Convention of 1925, but this was not ratified by the United States until the recent neutrality agitation and the adoption of an arms embargo by the United States for her own purposes. This treaty does no more than give such publicity to the arms trade of each state as the good faith of that state will provide. As the debates developed at Geneva, non-producing states were unwilling to give publicity to their imports unless producing states were willing to give publicity to their exports; the question turned, of course, upon national defense and strategy. The private trade in arms finally became absorbed in the whole question of disarmament, of which it is logically part.

Like disarmament, too, the problem of the private trade in arms is both a technical one and one of logic. It is war which produces the need for arms, and therefore leads men, whether for profits or for patriotism, to produce arms. If war is the method of achieving national aims, wars must be won; and to win wars there must be superiority in arms. Whether this superiority is attained by governmental manufacture or through private enterprise does not affect the issue of war in the least—except, perhaps, as to its successful outcome. To "remove the profits of war" is distinctly desirable from the viewpoint of national economy; but it will not remove war itself. The munitions trade is no more than a pimple upon the scaly monster of war; it is not the removal of the excrescence which is needed, but the destruction of the monster itself.

No plea is hereby made for the munitions trade. Reform in its methods is badly needed, and should be strenuously pressed. Senator Nye's investigation, it is to be hoped, will lead to some improvements; the danger is that we will accept this as a sufficient means of keeping us out of war. The only sense in which it can at all be maintained that the private manufacture of munitions leads to war is that they stir peoples to war through propaganda. But, even if this could be controlled, there are many other reasons given by recent writers for our entry into the World War. It is even conceivable that the people were not "misled," but honestly thought that certain ideals and certain interests were worth fighting for; there are some, indeed, who still think so.

And this is the heart of the matter. So long as peoples think that anything is worth fighting for, there will be a need for arms; and men have always believed that there are some things worth fighting for. They will continue to do so, and should continue to do so, if civilization is to survive and progress, until some other means than war is provided to assure them of the things which they think are important. To get rid of arms will not get rid of war; it will be easier to get rid of war than of arms.

CHAPTER IV

EDUCATION

Disarmament, in both of its phases just discussed, illustrates in its failure the importance of the principles laid down in the first chapter. It makes no effort to settle disputes, or to enforce rights, or to remedy wrongs. There are many other proposals to be tested by these criteria; and we shall take up first, among these, some more general ones which do not take into consideration these criteria. They approach the problem, and would solve it, in what seems a much simpler manner. In this and the following chapter two such proposals, which are allied, and which are widely accepted either separately or together, will be considered. In both cases, it seems fair to say, the thinker has been pushed back so far that he can find no other answer. No specific or concrete proposal satisfies him, and he desperately falls back upon idealistic solutions.

How often does a speech end, or an editorial, with a despairing plaint, such as that in the *New York World-Telegram* of December 9, 1935: "Education is the only way out. We must become civilized." Such statements are usually isolated; they rarely attempt to mark the road for us, to show how we may become civilized, to explain what education is, or what civilization is. When one studies how this education is to be achieved, one is apt to become even more despairing as to the possibility of eliminating war, if education is the only way out.

To begin with, what does this proposal intend? Most of those who hope to end war through education, it is to be suspected, think of it simply as educating the people to hate war. Over and over again this plea is heard. Preachers fulminate from their pulpits, and promise not to support a war again; lecturers from their platforms and over the radio tell of the horrible destructiveness of the next war and of the resulting collapse of civilization; the movies and books visualize for us the brutalities of war. The sum total of the message is that there must be no more war, and that, to assure that there will be no more war, people must be educated to dislike war. Apparently, it is the naïve belief of such persons that war, finding itself disliked, will immediately withdraw itself from the human scene. If this is the objective—merely to teach people to prefer peace to war—it seems safe to say that the task is already accomplished, and that their efforts are being wasted. It is, as was said at the beginning of this book, a work of supererogation. There can be no doubt that the people of this world, almost unanimously, would prefer to find some means other than war for accomplishing the things which they wish to have done. For the most part, education still teaches the duty of going to war for national purposes, and it will doubtless continue to do so; but this does not imply an approval of war. Those who oppose war find it necessary still to make use of war, until some better method of serving their purposes is found. And if it be not true that education has brought about a dislike of war, what more can be expected of the process of education than it now does? From every agency for education pours forth a flood of attack against the institution of war; it could not do more, if its objective is merely to arouse hate against war. Rarely is a voice raised in behalf of war; the condemnation of war is universal. Yet still we have war.

If, on the other hand, the purpose of this proposal is to educate human beings, or peoples, to such a point that there will be no discord, but only amity and goodwill between nations, it is necessary again to be pessimistic. A French political philosopher once asserted that the purpose of the state is to prepare the way for its own demise. By this he meant that the function of government is to teach its subjects respect for law, and to habituate them in respect for order to such a degree of perfection that every person would know, and knowing would respect, the rights of his fellows. When this had been accomplished, obviously there would be no further need for courts or policemen or legislatures, and government would then retire into oblivion. This, of course, is the ideal of philosophical anarchy—perhaps the most beautiful ideal that the human mind has ever imagined. Doubtless, too, it is the most hopeless. It implies omniscience on the part of each individual: he must know his rights in every situation present or future, in such absolute fashion that there is no possibility of disagreement with others, equally as omniscient. All persons must be infallible. It implies also a willingness to respect these rights, a charity and unselfishness on the part of every person in the world which in centuries of developing civilization we have not begun to approach as yet.

There is no doubt that the state has done much to teach its members the restraints on which civilization is founded; there is no doubt that far more persons know what rights to respect, within an increasing circumference of such rights, and are willing to cooperate rather than fight over these rights. But there are still numerous persons who have not learned to respect any rights; and there are continually new questions of rights for which education has not yet provided an answer, with the consequence that all persons are uncertain as to the rights which they should respect. In spite of all its centuries of experiences, the state is still far from that ideal stage at which disputes do not arise; or, if they do arise, can be settled peaceably by the parties to the dispute, without the necessity of outside coercion or judgment.

And if this be true within the state, with all its experience behind it, far less can it be expected that international government, hardly born as yet, can teach whole peoples to know and respect the rights of other peoples. Nations have had a much shorter period of cooperation; there has been an entire lack of governmental training from above; and their problem is many times intensified by mass psychology. Lord Raglan tells us that it must be centuries, by the most optimistic calculation, before the natives of Asia and Africa can be educated enough to solve the problems of world government; elsewhere he remarks that the peasants of Uganda are as enlightened as those of Southern Italy, or Andalusia. It was not necessary to confine his statement to such peoples; it will be centuries before any nation is educated to such a point of perfection. If one may judge by the relatively simpler problem of individuals, the education necessary to achieve the ideal of true anarchy will require an interminable period, as between nations; meanwhile, what shall be done to prevent the use of violence, or war, between nations?

It is important to note, also, that this educational process involves far more than a seat in a schoolroom. Individuals have been taught their civic duties by courts and policemen; the rights themselves have been stated by collective action. No objective answer is provided by Nature to these questions; thus far, we have had to depend upon collective human judgment, which is not always infallible, and which sometimes itself leads to disputes. Once the rights are stated, the uplifted club of the policeman in the background contributes largely in the training of individuals to respect these rights. It is probably correct to say that most persons would prefer peaceable settlement of their disputes, and are willing to respect rights collectively agreed upon; doubtless the policeman is necessary only for the anti-social minority. But so long as this minority is not restrained by the policeman, other persons are compelled to resort to force to defend themselves; coercion has been a necessary part of the educational process. This is the conclusion arrived at by Lord Raglan who, after the remarks above quoted, asserts that the only means of abolishing violence is by education, and that in education force must play its part.

If, then, it is intended that education should eliminate war by teaching people to hate war, it is wasted energy; if the intention is to eliminate war by teaching nations how to know and respect the rights of other nations, it may reasonably be called a hopeless effort. But if the purpose is to educate people concerning the methods, principles, and machinery through which war is to be prevented or controlled, then we are upon a different footing, though our problems are far from ended. It is upon this assumption that the present book is written; in this sense, it is projected as a part of the education necessary.

At this point, many questions arise. How is the campaign of education to be conducted? Shall it be an organized campaign, and if so, who is to direct it? If it is to be international in scope, it should presumably be supervised by an international authority. In this connection, it is to be observed that the League of Nations has a scheme of education which it asks its Members to pursue within their respective educational systems; though it should also be remarked that this is only a very small part of the entire program of the League for avoiding war. To many persons, however, such a supervised program would be regarded as an unpatriotic abnegation of national sovereignty; on the contrary, they would prefer to teach, and do teach in their national schools, that the state is the highest ideal in life, and that the state must achieve its desired ends at whatever sacrifice. By what authority can such teaching be declared wrongful? An internationally supervised plan of education would require a much stronger international government than we now have.

It is obviously impossible to go at it by command from above. Any scheme of education looking toward the elimination of war must necessarily be a voluntary one.

Dr. Boutelle Lowe has published a little brochure, entitled *International Education for Peace,* in which he outlines such a plan. It calls for unofficial propaganda and conferences, and for official action as follows: a national bureau of Peace Education in every country, and state and local bureaus as well, with instruction to be included in the public school programs; a division of Peace Education in various international organizations; official international conferences to arrange for an international Peace Day, to discourage propaganda inimical to peace, and to cooperate with other international movements such as the outlawry of war, or regulation of the munitions traffic. This is probably as reasonable a program as could be devised, and it would doubtless be of great help; yet it reduces itself, in final analysis, to unofficial efforts to stir up the people in each nation to establish the proposed national and international machinery.

And what is to be taught in this educational campaign? There is already in existence, and working in the general cause of peace, one of the most far-reaching propagandas in history. Hundreds of private organizations, and thousands of voluntary efforts, are spreading the cry of peace throughout the world. The programs of schools even now have much to say against war; and there are numerous international conferences, both official and unofficial, occupied with the problem. This effort could doubtless be intensified, along the lines above suggested; but it needs rather to be concentrated. At present, each organization propagates its own panacea or no solution at all further than to detest war, and goes merrily along its own way, barging into others, and dividing the anti-war movement into opposed camps.

This, probably, is the inevitable course of popular education. In the usual sense of classroom instruction, education is organized from above; it has therefore always the danger of being diverted to special and selfish purposes. Unorganized, it is a slow-moving and ponderous affair, apt to be led astray by demagogues and to be misshaped through lack of knowledge; ultimately, the public usually finds its way through the morass and onto solid ground. This is the course, probably, which must be taken by education opposed to war. Education organized from above, which might be more rapid and effective, presupposes the existence of an international government which it would require education to establish.

As to the value and importance of the educational process there can be no doubt. It is not only a means of ascertaining a proper course of action; in a democratic world it is a means of reaching decisions and establishing procedures. It has often been emphasized that no law can be properly effective unless it is supported by public opinion under its jurisdiction; a law, or a government, which is opposed by the bulk of public opinion is doomed to failure. Any plan to get rid of war, then, cannot be successfully established and maintained unless it has a respectable amount of support in public opinion.

But education alone is not sufficient. There are always some who do not get educated; there are always new problems arising which require a long time for their solution. We cannot hope to develop such perfect human beings that they will never dispute their rights, or that violence will never be used between them. There is nothing in the history of government over individuals to justify such a hope; there is less experience and less foundation for such a hope as between nations. Nor can education foresee and provide for all new situations as rapidly as they arise. Finally, even if education could do all this, it would require centuries to achieve it; meanwhile, what is to be done to stop war? The best that education can do is to seek out the proper means of controlling war, and to build up for it as much of a moral foundation and support as is possible. The more it can achieve in this direction, the more efficient will be the control established, whatever its nature. Every possible avenue should be pursued; intensive study should be given to every suggestion. Above all, this study should be objective; but to achieve this requires a whole campaign of education for itself. By far the most difficult part of educating people is to persuade them to think reasonably.

The objective of education must be, not a vague hope of idealizing mankind, but an established set of principles, a law, by which nations can be guided; a means of interpreting this law, in various situations; means of changing it, or adding to it, as new problems arise; and finally, means of compelling obedience to what the educated community demands, on the part of those who have not yet been educated to the point of respecting this law. Education is of fundamental importance but it is not a substitute for war; it is merely the preparation of a substitute, which must first be decided upon.

CHAPTER V

CAUSES OF WAR

Lord Raglan tells us that many pacifists have never considered "the fundamental causes of war and what, therefore, are the fundamental conditions of peace." War, he says, is a symptom of certain evils which must be remedied before the world can be made safe for peace. Others assert, more directly, that war can never be eliminated until the causes of war are ascertained and adjusted; their jeremiads sound much like those who demand education. They would abandon such fruitless things as international law and organization, and concentrate instead upon the task of removing the discontents which furnish the motives for war. As a matter of strict logic, this approach is impeccable; it commends itself further by its apparent ease; it has the double advantage of making war unnecessary (assuming that no state would ever enter upon an unnecessary war) and of providing satisfaction for everybody. It would lead to as happy a situation as that of the ideal of philosophical anarchy which we discussed earlier. It may be suggested, however, that it would be something of a task to remove all the causes of war; that a thoroughgoing international establishment would be necessary to achieve this end; and that, during the next few centuries while the work is being carried on, it would be desirable to provide some means of preventing the use of violence.

What are the causes of war? The question has not yet been answered in a fashion satisfactory to all, nor is it necessary for us to find an answer. There is enough material available for our purposes in the investigations of others. The Conference on the Cause and Cure of War has long studied the question, and it has been estimated that the Conference has by now discovered something over 250 causes. They have been grouped as psychological, economic, political, and social—which would seem to cover quite a large area of human activities. Tell A. Turner, in *The Causes of War and the New Revolution,* lists 41 causes, under the headings of economic, dynastic, religious, and sentimental, which widens the field a bit. Mr. C. F. Andrews adds race; Mr. G. A. Johnston adds industrial and labor causes. Others summarize the causes more simply as a desire for domination and a desire for gain. Sir Arthur Salter remarks that while there are many occasions for war, the causes may be classified as religious, dynastic, political, and economic; of these, the former two are now ineffective, and the political causes of war are increasingly inspired by economic causes. Mr. Bakeless also thinks that wars arise chiefly from economic causes. Mr. Wickham Steed, on the other hand, puts political causes first. Fear, he says, is the foremost cause for war: "The feeling of insecurity, and the fears which it engenders, are undoubtedly the strongest potential causes of war in the world today."

The Social Science Research Committee at the University of Chicago has for some years been conducting the most extensive research ever made into the causes of war. Its results thus far have been briefly summed up by its

Director, Professor Quincy Wright, in lectures delivered at the University of Geneva. His book is entitled *Causes of War and Conditions of Peace,* and this title, he explains, represents two ways of looking at the same thing. Indeed, he starts out with the "conditions of peace," which are: (1) a desire for peace superior to all hatreds, which means that there must be no intransigent oppositions; (2) an organization of the world community adequate to restrain conflicts; (3) a system of law intolerant of violence except as a legally controlled instrument of execution; (4) peaceful techniques for preventing extreme departures from an equilibrium of material forces in the states system (i.e., by violence). By turning these conditions of peace about, he arrives at the causes of war: (1) a state of opinion violently hostile to the existing state of affairs; (2) inadequacy of international organization to deal with conflicts; (3) inadequate system of law; (4) unstable equilibrium of material forces. Economics, he adds by way of explanation for its omission, enters into every aspect of war under this analysis; and the same is true of politics.

This analysis, which would be satisfactory to some thinkers, would be regarded as entirely inadequate by others, to whom economic discontents explain all wars. Many are attracted by the Communist argument, according to which capitalist society is continuously at war, sometimes merely on the economic level, sometimes through its political agents, which call upon armies and navies to make war. This situation results from the enormous amounts of capital which must find a place to grow, and which, to this end, must push into other countries. Since in every country there are capitalists, all faced with the same situation, it is inevitable that they should collide. When the capitalist economy is overthrown and replaced by a socialist economy, these basic conflicts which lead to war will no longer exist. Everything will then proceed according to a rational plan adjusted to the needs of members of society; and war will disappear because there will be no more causes of dispute. This is the way, and the only way, to get rid of war.

As to this argument, which has the virtue of simplicity in statement, there are a number of things to be said; and these things do not depend upon one's hatred of, or affection for, Communism, or Marxism, or Socialism. They would apply as well to Naziism, or to Fascism, or to democracy. The proletarian revolution offers little toward the solution of the problem of war. It is a dispute between classes, not between states; its frontier lines are horizontal, not vertical. There are disputes, apparently, even among Communists: Trotzky is in exile; in the United States many factions malign each other today. The argument above stated would be hotly disputed by various factions, each claiming to be the only authentic interpreter of Marx. And if these factions were states, they would doubtless be fighting each other through war instead of through pen and paper.

So long as there are states, so long will there be disputes between states, whether capitalists or communists control therein. Lord Lothian asserts that "sixty socialist sovereign states can no more be self-supporting than can sixty capitalist states. . . . The root of our economic as of our political troubles is the division of the world into sovereign states. Neither capitalism nor socialism can function until this anarchy is overcome." And even Norman Thomas (who has now come to oppose the League of Nations as the Communists have conversely come to support it) says: "nations are very unequal in size and resources, and even a Socialist nation will have need for raw materials outside its boundaries." If this be true, as it unquestionably is, then socialist nations would have the same sources of dispute between them as do capitalist nations. The proletarian issue is not one between states, but between individuals; it is not an international, though it might be a universal, issue. It is idle to say that human woes will disappear when the economic structure is rebuilt; it has been rebuilt on various occasions, usually with such an upset of the existing balance that war has followed.

The assumption behind the effort to remove the causes of war (when offered as a solution of the problem of war) is that it is possible to discover and remove all causes of human conflict; but there is no such panacea.

In the first place, there is no agreement as to what are the causes of war. If one may judge by the numerous suggestions above, a great variety of diseases affect the community of nations. Some diagnosticians speak of malevolent imperialism, others of hypochondriac nationalism; some states are overfat, some do not have enough carbohydrates. It is difficult to know, under these circumstances, just which evil to attack; the organ whose removal some seek would cause death if removed, according to the views of others. Certainly, this is what is disputed as to capitalism; but many would insist that there are causes of war other than economic—such as national pride, pure sentiment. And if such human characteristics as greed or fear are responsible for war, we shall have to develop psychology and psychiatry a long way before we can hope to handle them.

If it be replied that a proper study would reveal the causes of war, who would be called upon to make the study? It is much to be doubted whether the Communist groups would accept an investigation conducted by the social scientists of the University of Chicago. What Japan and Italy assert to be proper causes of war would not be so accepted by other nations. Democracy would probably protest bitterly—even to the point of war—if Fascists were to be assigned the right to decide what causes war; Fascists would as little like a Communist decision. The only answer is to find agreement among peoples as to who shall decide; and we are forced back to the need of an international government for the purpose.

The diagnosis of war is difficult; experts may and do disagree. But, supposing that there could be agreement, how could the causes be removed after it was agreed that these actually were the causes? Only, it is submitted, by an overwhelming and compelling authority. Those who call for preventive medicine forget that other types of remedy are often needed, such as strong purges, or even surgery. Preventive action is always desirable, but it is not always enough. It is not to be expected that those who are in possession will give up without a struggle. Norman Thomas says that "there would be no war for justice if injustice had not previously been established by the violence of those who sought profit from it." But how is this violence to be controlled except by a superior force? There will always be some who, even though they know the causes of war, will be ready to use violence if it is possible to do so for their own profit. To assume otherwise is to assume the beautiful but hopeless ideal of philosophical anarchy.

It will not be easy to resolve the ancient quarrel between the "haves" and the "havenots." There are always some who will seize what they can and hold it as long as possible; and this seems particularly true of nations. Within the state, with all its long experience, such persons have not been eliminated, though they have to a large degree been controlled. Some public utility companies use their power fairly; but since some of them exploit the people who depend upon them, it is necessary to regulate all public utility companies. The problem of an equitable distribution of wealth between individuals within a nation is far from solved; we have much less experience upon which to base a system of dividing the resources of the world between nations. The mere fact that one state has more than another may lead to war; and there will always be persons or states unwilling to accept what others think is a reasonable distribution. If the causes of war can be ascertained, there will always be states which are unwilling to alter the existing situation to their loss by adjustment of these causes. Indeed, this would be true of almost every state today. What, for example, would be the attitude of the United States, a "have" state? Many can only be made to do so by external compulsion; and again a powerful international system would be necessary to achieve these ends.

Nor can it be assumed that, at any given time, all the causes of war are known. If it were possible to remove all the causes of war today, a thousand new causes of war would appear tomorrow, and a thousand more the following day. A hundred years ago, no one thought of rubber or oil as potential causes of war; twenty years ago Communist and Fascist movements had not appeared to arouse fears and produce preparations for war. And if it be said that these are merely new manifestations of general and eternal principles, it remains true that we may anticipate such disputes over general principles in the future, in innumerable situations which are beyond our present capacity of imagination.

We have now on hand an ample supply of causes of war which we have thus far been unable to remove, and there is no doubt that others will be added as time moves along and circumstances change. Not all of the fogs of dispute are dissipated immediately upon the appearance of the sun of reason. It is too much to hope that the Communist Utopia—or a Fascist, or democratic, or any other—will appear, in which disputes would never arise. "There is little likelihood," says Mr. Thomas, "that by some miraculous agreement men will amicably remove the causes of war." What is to be done about war in the long period during which we seek out the causes of war, and the doubtless longer period while we endeavor to remove those causes? For here one approaches infinity! Shall we do nothing during this time?

There is no question as to the enormous importance

of discovering and removing the causes of dispute among human beings. Every success in this direction may mean the elimination of a potential war. Continuous and earnest study should be devoted to the effort, and along with it the development of a cooperative spirit on the part of individuals and of states. It is not enough to impose sanctions for prohibitive purposes only; there must be provided machinery for the revision of unjust situations. But it is precisely at this point that study is most needed. Those who would remove war by removing the causes of war do not tell us how to proceed. In all the centuries of its existence the state has not succeeded in eradicating the causes of dispute between individuals, so that the use of force between individuals should disappear; it is not to be expected that the community of nations can succeed in the same task merely by saying that the causes of war must be removed.

To remove the causes of war, a thoroughgoing international machinery is essential. There must be an authority to decide upon the causes; there must be an authority to determine the equitable adjustment in each case; there must be an authority to compel obedience to these decisions, as against the few who are always unwilling to submit. We cannot be content to scorn international organization and to substitute for it the causes of war; these causes cannot be removed except with the aid of a powerful international government. This has been the experience of human beings organized into states, and that experience cannot be disregarded. We must make every effort to remove the causes of war, but it is not enough to say it. That is equivalent to saying "let there be peace"; and we should have had peace long ago if that were enough. As a solution to the problem of war, the mere statement of the principle that causes must be removed is insufficient. It is a correct principle in itself, but the question remains: how are we to remove the causes of war? And that question is practically equivalent to asking: "how can we get rid of war?"

CHAPTER VI

PASSIVE RESISTANCE

Doubtless the simplest and most direct form of opposition to war is refusal to have anything to do with it. A few years ago the world was startled to hear that the Oxford University Union had approved, after debate, a motion that its members would not be willing to fight in a war on behalf of their country. The "Oxford Pledge" swept over the world; students everywhere took it up, and many who were not students. There are many organizations in the United States who take the attitude that the individual should refuse to go to war. Thus the War Resisters' League requires the following pledge from its members: "War is a crime against humanity. I therefore am determined not to support any kind of war, international or civil, and to strive for the removal of the causes of war." A similar position is taken by the Peace Patriots, the Fellowship of Reconciliation, the Women's Peace Union, the Women's Peace Society, and other organized groups. More recently, the Rev. Harry Emerson Fosdick, in a famous sermon, pledged himself never to support another war; and hundreds of preachers have followed his lead.

This, of course, is not a new idea, though its extension on such a wide scale is recent. Various religious groups have taken this attitude, in varying degrees, such as the Society of Friends, or the Mennonites. In many wars there have been conscientious objectors, increasing numbers of them; they have come to be recognized as a legal problem, and special provision has been made for them by military and judicial authorities. Thus far, it has been possible to treat them as exceptional cases; if the movement continues to spread, it will raise fundamental problems for government and society. Its recent growth may be ascribed to the mounting resentment against war, and to the increasing despair at the failure of the various current proposals for getting rid of war.

It must be observed, to begin with, that this attitude cannot be dismissed as mere cowardice. On the contrary, it requires a rare brand of courage to face ostracism by friends and neighbors, and the various cruel devices by which a community compels submission to its will. It may result in imprisonment, and even in death as a traitor. Those who refuse to go to war may face suffering and torture as great as they would find in war; they must have a deep and sincere belief to enable them to withstand the persecution which lies before them. One cannot quarrel with their courage; but it is possible to question their good judgment.

There is nothing simple in the problem of uprooting an institution so thoroughly established in the thought and habits of mankind as war; and the simple refusal to support war is not an answer. War is the use of force by states; one pledges himself, therefore, against the use of force by his nation. Obviously, the only way in which this can succeed is in persuading all peoples in all states to do the same thing; otherwise, the state which is willing to use force would have all others at its mercy. This situation would be admitted and accepted by many passive resisters; its consequences will be considered in a moment. Assuming, however, that there are some ideals or principles which humanity desires maintained, this position implies either that its followers bury their heads in the sand, as the ostrich is reputed to do, and refuse to look at what will happen; or else it implies the expectation that everyone can be brought, by some process, to that ideal state of which we have already spoken, in which no one will lift a hand against any other person. If the former, it is of course a foolish attitude which reasonable persons will disregard; if the latter, it faces the same problems which we encountered when discussing Education, or the Causes of War. Like both of these, it approaches philosophical anarchy, for it can only be completely successful when every person, or every state, has been trained not to resort to violence against another. With this as a *desideratum* there can certainly be no quarrel; but one may reasonably ask by what means a task up to now impossible is to be achieved, and meanwhile, until this happy stage is reached, what is to be done with those unreasoning persons who insist upon putting up their fists?

Passive resistance is frequently an emotional reaction, overwhelming in its strength, and requiring no justification on the part of the individual. In this form it cannot hope to succeed in preventing war; and various explanations have been offered. Some say that it is better to disobey than to commit murder; that the individual must choose between two immoral situations. This raises a question as to what is murder, for not every killing is a crime. If it were, we should be hard pressed to find policemen. The answer, of course, is that the use of force is a crime only when the community has decreed it to be; again, we are forced back upon the collective judgment of the community, and cannot be content with the judgment of the individual. Similarly, it is said that absolute pacifism is a moral equivalent for war, calling for the same virtues as war uses. If this refers to virtues within an individual, such as courage, it is doubtless true, but it is an equivalent only within his own bosom; if it refers to organization and discipline, the passive resistance movement has shown none of that as yet. When it does, it ceases to be an individual decision, and action taken must be decided upon and carried out by a collective system, in which the individual no longer decides.

The trouble with such arguments is that they are selfish and individualistic. They confront the problem from the viewpoint of the feelings of the individual person, and not from the viewpoint of the good of humanity. The individual dislikes—who does not?—the thought of inflicting pain and perhaps death upon another; he therefore selfishly says that he will not be guilty of it. Thus he arrogates to himself the right to decide what is right or wrong, what is bad or worse; or else he refuses to share in maintaining what the community thinks is right. He disregards the duty of helping his fellow whenever such help involves the use of force; rather than pain himself or violate his own beliefs, he would permit a crime to be done against his neighbor which he could prevent by using force against the criminal. In this light, the absolute pacifist is anti-social; he is concerned only with himself and his own feelings. He is, in international affairs, an anarchist (where, of course, he has plenty of company, of various kinds); and it is difficult to see why his reasoning would not lead him in domestic affairs as well, to deny the right of the community to employ force for its ends.

Such a person may find a moral equivalent for force to replace the savage instincts within himself; but he contributes no moral equivalent for force as a means of protecting rights or remedying wrongs. Nor can it be assumed that wars are due simply to the fighting instincts within man, and that if these instincts can be replaced within each person by loftier feelings, there would be no further occasion for war. He must, in the first place, convert everyone else; but after he has done this—which is another problem—it may yet remain true that lofty ideals may seek to impose themselves by force upon other lofty ideals, and that the latter must resist by force. History is not lacking in illustrations. War, that is to say, may be sought for other reasons than the ferocious instincts inherent in man; and the sublimation of those instincts, even in every human being, would not necessarily rid us of war.

We are, as a matter of fact, now approaching the heart of the problem of war. Granted that enough persons would take a pledge not to fight in another war, which is doubtful when one considers that it must be done in every state; and granted that these persons, when war breaks out, should live up to their pledge, which also seems improbable when one recalls the last war; granted all this, it seems reasonable to say that there would be no war. If no one will fight, then there will be no fight.

But also, there will be no solution. War, we said, is

a method, a means to an end; the end has frequently been unjustified, but sometimes it has been, and sometimes in the future it may be, an important end. It may be necessary to right a wrong, or to protect an established right, or to do something else which human beings think worth while. Passive resistance destroys the means, but it does not achieve the end; it offers no substitute for the means which it eliminates. Its force is spent when it has prevented war; it has no energy left for the necessary building. It is purely destructive, not constructive; it is negative, not positive. It prevents the use of force to settle a dispute; it also prevents the settlement of the dispute. The party in possession remains in possession; there is no way to compel him to surrender or to compromise. From this dilemma, passive resistance cannot escape; unless it serves justice, it maintains injustice. Unless it provides a substitute for war as a means to these ends, it obstructs progress; and it offers no such substitute, unless in different form, to be discussed in a moment. The simple refusal of individuals to fight in a war may stop or diminish bloodshed, but it does not advance humanity. If there were peaceful means—education, anarchy, or other—to induce those who do wrong to repair that wrong, there would be no need for war, and no need for passive resistance. But we have not yet reached that happy stage of existence; there are still many, whether persons or nations, who are willing to take advantage of their fellows, and who can only be restrained from doing so by the exercise of superior force. Passive resistance removes this superior force and leaves the criminal, who is willing to use force, in undisputed control.

The answer which some absolute pacifists would make to this argument is that peace is more important than justice; and here, indeed, we arrive at the very core of the problem of war. Is there anything more important than peace? Certainly so, says history—men have always been willing to fight for their ideals; so civilization has been builded. They have fought for liberty, and for other things; but always they have been willing to fight, and to maintain domestic government supported by overwhelming force, to uphold justice. The same affirmative answer is given by political experience, which has cumulatively shown the necessity for combining the might of all against the illegality, the criminality, of the few. For this purpose the state has created and authorized the policeman to use force; and where the policeman is not available, human beings will fight—individually, or in riots, or in civil wars—for what they conceive to be their rights. As between nations, the lesson of this political experience is only now being put into effect; but passive resistance would deny it at once. How can passive resistance deny the right to use force to maintain order between states, while affirming its use within the state?

To the absolute pacifist—if he has really thought the matter out—peace stands above all else; to others, passive resistance means the surrender of things which they regard as important. Even so, it is argued, peace is better than using war and losing life for those things. One might live as happily under George VI, or the Mikado of Japan, or even under Herr Hitler. But the process would not stop here. The unscrupulous would soon recognize and take advantage of the submissive attitude of those who pursue the method of passive resistance. Not only would individual persons, or national groups, be forced to submit to a disagreeable yoke; more important than that, the ethical principles, the legal norms, the habits of conduct builded up through painful centuries of social and political experience—all would be lost. Those who wish for decent relations between human beings would have abdicated in favor of those who do not. The declaration that force will not be used against force leaves force supreme.

Consider some concrete examples. There are fifteen or twenty states in the world today which have taken on a dictatorial government in some form. Suppose that these states should combine against the democratic states. Should the latter—should the people of the United States —refuse to fight in a war against this combination? If peace is most important, there should be such a refusal; but many persons who have signed a pledge not to support another war would find themselves much embarrassed in that situation. If Fascism won, and we were submitted to it, doubtless we could make a living; is there anything else worth fighting for? Liberty of thought, of religion, of speech? equality of rights? democracy? It might be suggested that passive refusal to submit to the commands of the new government would prove so embarrassing for the new rulers that they would desist. But this would mean cessation of constructive effort, diminution of production, and probably as much persecution and human misery as would come from war—aside from the fact that human ingenuity could be used against as well as by passive resistants.

Or turn the situation round. Suppose the situation were actually as the late Frank Simonds put it, and the world were divided into the "haves" and the "havenots"—a few states controlling most of the territory and resources of the world, and many others unable to secure the necessities of life for their peoples. It may be a little difficult for Americans, who "have," to conceive such a situation; but if you can imagine yourself as a "havenot," would you be content to suffer, or would you prefer to use force to demand your share of the gifts of nature? We are assuming that no other power of sufficient authority is in existence to do this for you—that point will be taken up later in our discussion. At this moment, three of the "Great Powers" of the world take the position that since the community of nations provides no peaceful method by which their needs can be supplied, they must depend upon the use of their own force. Here is a case in which passive resistance would be futile—against whom would the resistance be directed? To resist by passive acceptance of the situation would gain nothing.

To the above argument, it would be replied by some that passive resistance is not entirely barren, but that, like its alternative, force, it can be made positive or constructive, as well as negative. It is a new method, and would require much study to find the proper means of application in each particular case; but it is not beyond human ingenuity to discover these means. Gandhi, they would say, not only resisted superior force, but compelled it to take action along desired lines. At this point, we begin to speak in terms of "non-violent coercion" rather than in terms of "passive resistance."

To many persons, the success of Gandhi is the answer to all problems. There are undoubtedly cases in which a purely negative resistance may bring positive results; and there is no doubt that along these lines Gandhi has had a remarkable success. There is also no doubt that his success was due to the emotional appeal aroused among his followers by his own personality, and that no one else in history has had his success. But how are we to find a Gandhi each time that we need him; and how are we to be sure that he leads in the right direction when we have found him? Would he have had such success in the United States? Or would it be Father Coughlin, or Townsend, or Father Divine? Should we elect him or appoint him, or should he take a civil service exam, or should we simply wait for God to call him?

Gandhi is a phenomenon, not a method. Scientists have in the past explained phenomena in terms of natural laws, and reduced them to our use; perhaps we shall some day do the same with the Gandhi phenomenon. At present, however, we do not know the answer. Mr. Frank Olmstead, of the War Resisters' League, in a recent issue of the *National Student Mirror* says: "The only hope of preventing another world conflict is for some national leader of outstanding importance to appeal to the peoples of the world in a clarion call for faith in justice instead of war. . . . If the chances seem slim that any such prophet of sanity should appear, and if the response to his appeal seems doubtful, it is because we are in a desperate situation." But surely, that is when we most need the leader! For our purposes, such a leader would have to be an international figure, with a following in all the states which might go to war; if he were to appear in one state only, his success might mean only the more rapid conquest of his own state by the other belligerent, in which no Gandhi had appeared.

If passive resistance is to mean anything more than a subjective decision on the part of each individual concerning war, it must be organized; and once this conclusion is reached, many of the difficulties which we have encountered hitherto will be repeated. The argument that passive resistance, or non-violent coercion, is a weapon which can be used with as positive results as can the weapon of war, deserves consideration. It implies in the first place attack or attempted control, since there must be something to resist. It would seem, therefore, to be useless except as against actual aggression; it would serve none of the purposes or functions of war except that of self-defense. Except where there is aggression, it would not serve to settle a dispute, to remedy a wrong, or to enforce a right.

If it be contended that non-violent coercion can be used as a positive method or weapon, like war, then it can be used to serve bad as well as good purposes; and if it is to replace war, then the question must be asked concerning it, just as truly as concerning war: to what end shall it be employed? and who is to determine this? If it should fall into the hands of a Coughlin or a Hitler, it may not accomplish so praiseworthy an end as in the hands of a Gandhi or a Kagawa. If it should prove to be a successful method of social control, there is no doubt that efforts would be made to seize upon it and prostitute it to selfish ends, just as has been done with the use of force, or war.

The question of organization and direction therefore becomes of great importance.

When one asks the question whether peace is to be preferred to justice the *riposte* often comes back: what is justice? did you ever hear of a just war? But this question must be asked, equally, concerning non-violent coercion. Who knows whether it will or does advance justice? The answer, thus far, has always been in the mind of the conscientious objector himself, as an individual; yet here he is asking for mass action. As a single person, he is not willing to kill his fellow man, or he does not think the war is worth fighting. But how can others know that he is right? There may be other pacifists who oppose his view, with the result that passive resistance would fight against passive resistance—surely the *reductio ad absurdum!*

There is no absolute or ideal criterion for justice; but it is clear that it is impossible to permit each individual to decide for himself what is justice. The best that humanity has been able to do thus far is to accept the decision of the organized community of which it is part. The community, through its accepted organs, states the law and interprets the law; thus it administers justice. This is the best that humanity has yet been able to do toward establishing justice; it is certainly better than allowing each individual or each nation to decide for itself; that would give to the criminal a free hand. Passive resistance cannot determine what justice is; before it can do so, it must be organized. For that matter, it cannot hope to be effective for whatever objective it may have, unless it has organization to direct its efforts. At best, it can only maintain the *status quo;* and this the average human would dislike. He wants change; the ideal of progress is ever before him. Peace is not merely the absence of war.

If, then, we regard passive resistance as individual refusal to fight in war, it is anti-social, since it puts the judgment of the individual above the judgment of the group, and refuses to share in the collective responsibility agreed upon by the group. If, on the other hand, passive resistance, or non-violent coercion, is to be regarded as a method or weapon which can, as effectively as does war, achieve positive results toward justice and human advancement, then it cannot be trusted to individual nations who might abuse it as they have abused war; it must be taken over by the community of nations, and organized under the control of the community. Whether war or passive resistance is the method, the well-being of the individual can be advanced only if the method has the proper objective, and only if the method is properly organized and controlled. In either case—or whatever the method—the members of the community must agree upon what is desirable and must jointly retain control over whatever methods of coercion are employed.

Yet there is a common ground upon which some pacifists, at least, and those who believe in an international government, can stand together. The absolute pacifist may take and observe his pledge never to support another war; but he runs contrary to all human experience if he defines war to include every use of force. Such a definition would not, indeed, be regarded as correct in international law. When force is employed by an organized community to maintain its law, such force is not illegal or immoral; when force is employed by the organized community of nations to maintain its law, it is not war but police action—currently called sanctions. And from this viewpoint, war as instrument of national policy should be illegal and prohibited. The supporter of the military sanctions of an international government could if he wished, equally with the pacifist, take a pledge never to support another war, for war, in international law, is the use of force by one state against another, and does not refer to the organized and authorized use of force by the community of nations to maintain peace and order within the community. The pacifist, if he can accept the use of force by a policeman under domestic law, should be able to interpret his pledge against war to accept the authorized use of force under the law of the community of nations. The two positions are far apart; but they can find common ground in the acceptance of the community judgment which mankind has always found to be essential. That judgment should refuse to support war as an instrument of national policy and should at the same time be willing to support international police action.

But peace, in the sense of mere passivity, is a sterile concept; peace is worth while only as an organized and constructive effort to advance human well-being. It can never be obtained merely by refusing to participate in the use of force.

CHAPTER VII

THE OUTLAWRY OF WAR

The first function of any government is to suppress violence. Whenever there is general objection to any procedure within the state, the first thought of the citizen is to pass a law declaring it illegal. With such habits of thought it would seem natural to declare war illegal in the international community; yet that idea is scarcely a decade old. It is an American idea; it appears to have originated with some sincere friends of peace who had despaired of Wilsonian ideas and had struck out in other directions. As far back as 1922, Senator Borah had introduced into the Senate a resolution embodying the idea that war is a crime; other prominent people supported it; and soon the American people, with their usual slavery to slogans, took up the cry to outlaw war with enthusiasm, but without understanding.

For the movement is not so simple as it sounds. The principle itself, that war should be declared illegal, deserves the most sincere praise. No more important contribution has ever been made to the problem of eliminating war; even in the sum total of human experience it will rank as one of the most significant contributions ever made. If it seems surprising that the idea had not appeared earlier, one should reflect that there was no international government which could, until recently, enunciate such a law. States had for centuries been accustomed to taking care of their own rights and interests; indeed, the doctrine of sovereignty had developed the belief that there was nothing higher than the state in human affairs. So long as the state was the limit of the horizon, no one was able to look beyond.

The increasing interdependence of states has gradually diminished the importance of national sovereignty, and human beings have become more and more accustomed to the necessity of cooperation between states, which implies that states must submit to common rules. But the use of of violence weakens the possibility of cooperation. War had been accepted as one of the plagues of mankind, along with earthquake, fire, and the like. International law had whittled at war, through treaties for pacific settlement of disputes, through rules for the conduct of war, and otherwise; but law had not attempted to control the use of war itself. With the appearance of international organization and a sense of collective security, it was not difficult to take the next step, and propose that war itself be declared illegal.

It was none the less a revolutionary step. War has long been the supreme attribute of the sovereign state—the method by which it has sought to advance its own interests, to settle its own disputes, to enforce its own rights or its own wishes. The right to make war is obviously the antithesis of the reign of law. If, then, war were forbidden, the sovereign state was deprived of its right to resist the rule of law; the necessary implication was an authority outside of states to state and enforce the law, and it must be a powerful authority. No more revolutionary change has been proposed in political history; its consequences are far-reaching and profound.

But the leaders of the outlawry of war movement refuse to recognize these consequences, and have thereby, thus far, nullified the entire effect of the proposal. They have, in fact, made use of an acceptable proposal, of wide appeal, to propagate beliefs of their own which have no logical derivation from the principle which they promulgate. To the average American, the word "outlaw" connotes a person outside the law, with a policeman or posse in continuous pursuit. But the leaders of the outlawry of war movement assert that there is no place for a police to enforce obedience on the part of sovereign nations. They state the rule; they then deny and reject any means of enforcing the rule. This interpretation of the slogan the average follower does not realize, and he is misled as a result. It is probably true that the average supporter of the slogan has not attempted to think what it implies; it sounds good, as it really is, in itself. But if he does stop to think about it, he is confronted with this dilemma: either the slogan consists of meaningless words, or the words must be backed up with proper authority. He has only to draw upon his own experience to know that the mere writing of words upon a statute book does not make them effective as law. Whether or not, in legal philosophy, they deserve to be called law, need not concern us here. The point is that the average citizen who has fallen in behind the slogan "outlaw war" does not realize that the slogan is interpreted by its makers as a mere *fiat,* and that these makers deny that force should be employed to make the law effective. He has heard the words, and he interprets them according to his own habits of thought—without, perhaps, following them out to their logical conclusion. But the average American is not so gullible as to believe, after he has paused to think, that violence can be restrained by merely shouting a slogan, or even by writing it into a treaty.

Dr. Charles Clayton Morrison, who is the exponent of the movement (The Outlawry of War, Chicago, 1927), recognizes this situation, but claims that the pragmatic attitude is to base world organization for peace upon the plighted faith of nations, and upon that alone. For this position, he offers three arguments: (1) existing relationships of international understanding rest and always have rested upon mutual good faith; (2) there is no conceivable alternative to the plighted word; (3) the plighted word has far greater value and potency than a system which provides for or presupposes war.

The first of these arguments simply begs the question. Treaties have been fairly well observed in the past, partly because they have never attempted to impose upon sovereign states such vital restrictions as prohibiting the use of war, partly because behind many of them there has been the fear of coercion. But if it were true that treaties are sufficiently well observed, than there would be no need for the improvement which the world is so desperately seeking today. If treaties were properly obeyed, then we should have no wars. The Pact of Paris alone, which is founded upon the plighted faith of nations, would be sufficient to avert war; and there are many other treaties in existence which would do the same, if they were properly obeyed. But recent happenings, without looking back over the pages of history, are sufficient to disprove this reasoning. One after another, important treaties have been violated—by Japan, by Germany, by Paraguay and Bolivia, by Poland, and by Italy. How can it be said, after this enumeration, that the plighted faith of nations is sufficient? It never has been, and is not now, enough.

This being so, it would be a hopeless world if Dr. Morrison's second argument were correct—that there is no other alternative to the plighted word. We may accept the plighted word as the beginning of human agreement; but certainly it does not have to be the end thereof. If such an agreement were made by a small group, for particular national purposes, such as the old offensive and defensive alliances, it might be expected to operate only so far as the selfish purposes of its signatories dictated. If, however, it were an agreement between all states, for the purpose of maintaining principles of value to all and accepted by all, the situation would be quite different. Enough states would have an interest in maintaining the agreement to oppose the one state, or the few states, which might wish to disregard it; these states might, indeed, be willing to use their common strength to compel obedience to the accepted rules of the community. The universality of such a system would discourage any one state from disobedience; the combined force of all would usually include a strength sufficient to coerce dissidents; the sacrifice required of each for this purpose would be small, since divided, and willingly given since for a common purpose. This, at any rate, has been the experience of human beings within the state, and it has been fairly successful. A law must have general consent before it can be effective; with this general consent it is possible to establish an authority which can compel observance of the agreement on the part of malcontents and dissidents. The possibility of a cleft between equal groups—civil war—is undeniable; we are talking of human beings, and we do not expect perfection.

The third argument implies that forcible sanctions are war—a misconception which destroys the argument. They may be force, they may be violence; but they are not war. And if such use of force were war, then it might be necessary to employ war. Force may be used for various ends—some of them good, some of them bad. When it is used by a community, through its proper agents and under its proper authority, to maintain the rules agreed upon in that community, force is put to a good use; this has never been denied within the state, and can no more be denied within the community of nations. War has come to mean the use of force by a state for its own purposes, which may be good or bad; but this is a very different thing from the use of force by the community of nations in behalf of all. That particular use of force which we call war has been condemned by public opinion throughout the world and has, though imperfectly, been declared a violation of international law; but the use of force by the organized community of nations, in behalf of the whole community, corresponds to the use of force within a state by the policeman. So long as nations may use force for their own purposes, it may accomplish no more than does the plighted word of nations; but when it is used to establish the reign of law within the community of nations, it is the necessary support of this plighted faith against those who fail to respect their oaths.

The outlawry of war movement, then, is content to say that war is illegal, and do no more about it. It has called upon public opinion and, with the aid of the League of Nations, rallied the most imposing popular denunciation against war by Japan and by Italy that has ever been seen, and wholly in vain. Yet the slogan has an appealing simplicity, and the American people who ardently desire peace—though without paying for it—were bemused by the siren voices, and forgot to take reason with themselves.

It was in this atmosphere that the Pact of Paris was born. No commitments were desired; no effort was to be made; no price whatever was to be paid for the greatest boon which could be imagined for the human race. The Pact of Paris does not formally declare war illegal; its signatories merely renounce it as an instrument of national policy, and agree not to seek a settlement of their disputes except through pacific means. The interpretations which accompanied it, and which guide the conduct of its signatories, admitted that war in self-defense was legitimate, and that each state could say for itself that it was fighting in self-defense. International lawyers are unable to find in the Treaty any legally binding rule against war; one of them even goes so far as to assert that this treaty for the first time in history makes war legal. This is so, he argues, because international law had never before admitted war to be legal, but had accepted it as an unavoidable fact, whereas the Pact of Paris admits all wars of self-defense as legal, and then makes it possible to call any war a war of self-defense. This exception, of course, vitiates the treaty.

This is not to deny that the Pact of Paris promulgates the most important principle ever put forward for the benefit of the human race, nor that public opinion throughout that world has accepted it fervently. It is probably the greatest document of history, and its potentialities are unlimited. But it has not, as it stands, been enough to stop a war. It did not suffice to prevent the use of violence between Russia and China in 1929; nor the Japanese attack on China in 1931; nor the struggle between Paraguay and Bolivia; nor had it had the slightest effect upon Italy. It has proved so helpless in these recent cases, its only tests, that it has become an object of ridicule, and statesmen hesitate to invoke it. Plighted faith, put into words on paper, has proved impotent to stop war, the outlawry of war movement to the contrary notwithstanding.

Disarmament and the Kellogg Pact are the two great gestures toward world peace made by the United States to satisfy the clamor of her people for a contribution toward peace, since they are unwilling to accept the method established by the remainder of the world. Like the present attempt at a new neutrality, they are escape mechanisms. They have failed—as they unquestionably have—because they offer no substitute for war, no method of achieving the ends which nations believe can be achieved by war. Toward the settlement of disputes the Kellogg Pact does more than disarmament could, for it at least enunciates a negatively stated obligation not to seek a settlement except by pacific means. This, of course, does not require any state to seek a settlement. If it is satisfied, or if it is illegally in possession, it is protected; the claimant state is obligated to use only pacific means toward obtaining a settlement, even though the other state may refuse entirely to submit the dispute to settlement. Long before the Kellogg Pact came into existence there were more effective treaties for compelling states to seek a pacific settlement. It is a paper pledge; it has no obligation, no machinery, no authority. It does not provide a means for settling disputes.

Nor does it make any effort, even the slightest, to provide for the remedying of injustices, or for enforcing rights. Yet these are functions, as we have before noted, which are indispensable in a human society. And there was in existence, before this Pact, machinery for the performance of these functions much more effective than was provided in the Pact; indeed, it provided none. When one compares the Pact of Paris with this machinery, inadequate as it is, one is forced to wonder at the motives and purposes of the statesmen who made it, and the extent to which they had their tongues in their cheeks as they signed.

But, whatever may have been the motives of the statesmen, who knew what they were doing, there is no doubt that peoples everywhere, who did not understand the situation fully, intended to make a contribution toward peace; and there can be no doubt, too, that they did make a great contribution in principle, even though it is not yet mechanized and implemented. They did not realize that this principle would not work by itself; many of them were not aware of the fact that it was emasculated by its leaders in advance. Most of them, doubtless, did not think of the possibility that some sacrifice might be necessary in order to make the outlawry of war effective. By now, they should realize this; the question is now whether they are willing to get behind it with more than the words which have proven so vain, and to provide means of obtaining respect for it. Certainly, it would be tragic for so important a principle as this to remain idle.

If war is to be outlawed, it must be driven out of the law; but, asks Madariaga, what law? It must be international law, and this law must be made by international society. This is admitted by the outlawry of war movement, which concedes also that there must be an international court. Thus it has recognized two of the three essential functions of government—the legislative and the judicial (though they are not provided for in the Pact)—but it denies what every government considers as essential—an executive power. Why is it omitted? If for the reason that it is unnecessary, we have already seen that this is an impotent reason. If, as some would argue, because national sovereignty should not be submitted to direction and compulsion, then the possibility of law and order is denied, and peace is made impossible.

Or it may be argued that force should not be employed against states. This may derive from the extreme pacifist view that force should never be employed in human relations, or it may derive from the assertion that such use of force is merely the war which we are trying to eliminate. The former we have considered. As to the latter, it may be noted that the outlawry of war movement concedes the right to make war or use force in self-defense, with each state being the judge of what is self-defense. If war or force can be used for this purpose, why can it not be used for other worthy purposes? Self-defense is not always confined within one's own territory, nor is it always passive. One may be forced to take the aggressive—in the sense of first attack—in order to defend one's person or property. Indeed, the Kellogg Pact permits any war to be fought under the cloak of self-defense; why, then, should not force be used by the organized society of nations to remedy wrongs and to enforce rights? If force is to be used, surely it should be used for the benefit of all rather than for the selfish interests of separate states.

It is to be hoped that such a use of force would rarely be needed; there might be efficacious methods short of military action to supply the coercion sometimes needed. But whatever the method employed, it is clear that it represents no advance until it is put into the hands of the organized society of nations; if it is left in the hands of individual states, we have as little hope for peace and justice as there has been in the past.

CHAPTER VIII

NEUTRALITY

Recently, in discussions of the problem of war, the word neutrality has come to play an important part. For several centuries, neutrality has been regarded as a technical field of international law, in which the average citizen could have no direct interest. It is slowly being recognized now that the question of neutrality is fundamental in the community of nations, and that it involves profound questions of morals and political philosophy as well as puzzling questions of practical politics and law. So far as the United States is concerned, it is doubtless the most important question of foreign policy that will ever face her people. It is a complicated and difficult matter, from some aspects; but it can be reduced to some simple though fundamental issues.

In a broad sense, neutrality means refraining from taking sides in a dispute between others. In its historical development, however, it became a matter of establishing the relative rights of neutrals and belligerents, and of stating the duties which each had in this status of impartiality. The neutral, of course, wished to continue his ordinary activities as little disturbed as possible by the existence of a war between other states; the belligerent, in his anxiety to win the war, wished to interfere with any and all neutral activities which might be of benefit to his enemy. In this struggle, the neutral was always at a disadvantage, for he was unprepared and did not wish to fight, while the belligerent was already armed and ready to take every allowable advantage of the neutrals' indisposition for fighting. Neutrals did, however, during the course of these centuries, put up a resistance to the pretensions of belligerents sufficient to produce the compromise which we call the international law of neutrality, as of August, 1914.

It is no part of our purpose to study the technicalities of this law, but we shall need to state enough of them to help reveal its connection with the elimination of war. A neutral government was not itself allowed to supply anything to either belligerent; but it had no responsibility for preventing such supply by individuals from within its territory. On the other hand, these individuals had certain restrictions put upon them by the law of neutrality. If they attempted to sell materials of actual military use, such as guns and gunpowder, their shipments might be captured and legally confiscated as absolute contraband by the belligerent. There were other articles which were classified as conditional contraband, and could be confiscated if destined to military use. And finally, there were other goods which were non-contraband, and not subject to capture, such as food destined for civilian use. These categories were based in part upon a distinction between combatants and non-combatants. The belligerent had a right also, to stop all trade with his enemy through the use of a blockade, provided it was an effective one. During the World War, blockade was extended, and contraband lists as well, to include neutral states adjacent to the enemy, on the theory that goods might be transshipped from this neutral to the enemy.

This was the law which was supposed to apply when the War broke out in 1914. But even by that date times had changed; and they have changed much more since then, to the increasing detriment of the neutral. In the first place, the character of war itself had changed. The conduct of a modern war calls for many things besides guns and gunpowder. An army in the field needs all sorts of motorized transport, and rubber for its wheels, and oil to make it move. It requires complete railway lines behind the trenches, and telegraph and telephone lines as well. Mules were of importance to Italy in Ethiopia. Copper, cotton, and especially oil, become of prime importance; and many other things as well. Even lipsticks were contraband in the World War, for they contain glycerine from which high explosives are manufactured.

The situation is further complicated by the fact that in a modern war the entire population is put to war uses. Women and children will be conscripted for the next war; it is a fact that a sixteen-year-old girl working in a munitions factory a thousand miles behind the battle lines may contribute as much, if not more, toward winning the war, than the soldier with a gun in the trenches. Consequently, the old distinction between combatant and non-combatant tends to disappear; and that part of the law of neutrality which is founded on that distinction disappears with it. The result is that everything formerly classified as conditional contraband now becomes absolute contraband; and even non-contraband materials, perhaps including food for civilian use, will be stopped if possible because all civilians are now engaged in war services. This means that practically all neutral trade with belligerents will be stopped, and not only with belligerents; trade with other neutrals which might eventually reach the enemy will likewise be stopped.

What is the neutral to do in this new situation? The only way he has been able to maintain his rights in the past was to fight for them, as the United States did in her two greatest wars. Even so, it is practically an impossible task. In the World War, we should have had to fight both the belligerents, if we really wished to uphold our rights as neutrals; indeed, we should have had to fight ourselves as well, for after we entered the War we assisted in doing the very things to which we had objected before our entry. The old war of neutrality would have to be entirely rebuilt if used in the next war; and even then it could be maintained only by the combined strength of the neutrals against the belligerents. Times have changed!

And times have changed elsewhere as well. Modern interdependence makes it impossible to conduct a war without importing materials for war use. Even the self-sufficient United States must import a dozen or more materials for war use, which she does not produce herself. The belligerent, then, is much more dependent than formerly on the neutral. On the other hand, the neutral is much more affected by any war than before, as the excitement over a colonial adventure in Africa now shows. It is no longer possible for the neutral to say: "Let them fight; it does not affect us." Any war, anywhere, affects all neutrals.

This new situation has been recognized in the community of nations; and its recognition has led to further developments, of even greater importance in the problem of neutrality. It is a development which turns our minds toward law and political science, and far deeper, into field of morals and philosophy. The community of nations, largely to deal with this problem, has become organized, and has taken the control of war under its own authority. The Kellogg Pact announces, in principle at least, that war is illegal; the League of Nations establishes machinery and law for its control. The United States is not a member of this organization, but they are very much affected by it. For the League of Nations abandons the principle of neutrality, and establishes instead the principle of collective responsibility, under which each state has a duty not to be impartial in a war. On the contrary, its Members must show partiality toward the state which obeys the law of the community, and must oppose the state which disobeys that law. Obviously, when the vast majority of states abandon the principle of neutrality, it becomes difficult, and even dangerous, for other states to attempt to continue a policy of neutrality.

These new developments force us to reconsider the question of neutrality, and we are led at once into fundamental discussions. There is first the moral issue. Probably every system of ethics demands that human beings should stand up for the right as against the wrong; that is the teaching of the Christian religion, certainly. It is the lesson also of political experience, which shows us that the right has been, and can be, maintained only by the combined efforts of all against the wrongdoer. It is for this reason that governments exist, and that individuals are willing to make some sacrifice of their liberty and some efforts toward the common needs. If, then, we base our conclusions upon morals, or upon the more practical foundation of political action, neutrality in the face of human conflicts appears inconsistent with the past experience of humanity.

These principles apply as well between states, which are aggregates of human beings, as between individuals. When a state declares its neutrality, it says in effect: "What do we care which side wins? Am I my brother's keeper?" The result is that might makes right; and if this does not concern a particular state in a conflict between Japan and China, or between Italy and Ethiopia, it may concern them in another struggle. England was willing to be neutral as between China and Japan but she was eager to have other states forget their neutrality and come to her aid when her interests were more directly affected in Northern Africa. But help is not apt to be given to a state in her difficulties if she is unwilling to help other states in their difficulties. This principle of reciprocal aid has long governed human conduct; it is as applicable between states if they wish to preserve law and order as between themselves.

Aside from moral values and practical advantages, it is generally conceded by experts today that neutrality is impracticable, if not impossible. It can be regarded as a useful compromise in earlier days, but modern conditions make it unworkable. As we have seen, the belligerent depends upon the neutral, and the neutral is affected by whatever the belligerent does. To such an extent is this true that the belligerent must depend more than ever on the neutral, and the neutral must endure more or must fight more than ever. The pressure is too great for the belligerent to pay respect to the law unless he is forced to do so. Also, however scrupulously impartial the neutral may wish to be, he is sure no matter what he does to injure one belligerent more than the other. When the United States, in the World War, asserted that she would sell equally to Germany and to her allies, the actual result was that Germany could obtain nothing from the United States. Had the situation been reversed, had we refused to sell to both sides, our neutrality would have offset the British navy to the advantage of the Germans. When we refused to sell to both Italy and Ethiopia, the result was actually to hurt Italy more than Ethiopia; for Ethiopia could not obtain supplies from us anyhow; but if Ethiopia were next door to us, she would suffer more in comparison, since Italy has more resources of her own. Neutrality cannot be impartial today, if it ever could; its inevitable result in the situation of our day is to weaken the weaker state, and to help the stronger state to win.

Not only this, but the exercise of neutrality has become positively dangerous. As the belligerent depends more on the neutral, he demands more of the neutral. He refuses —as both sides did during the World War—to be bound by "antiquated" rules of neutrality. The neutral can only maintain his usual intercourse with other states—already unduly limited by the legal rights of belligerents during war—if he is willing to fight for them. Nothing else will daunt the belligerent, who feels that he has too much at stake, in the way of national honor or even existence.

The alternative is to refuse to maintain neutral rights; and this principle has been considered by the Congress of the United States, and to some extent embodied in law. It is hoped to escape being drawn into war by removing all possible causes of friction with belligerents; and this is to be done by keeping at home all American citizens and their ships and their property. By staying at home they do not risk being captured, and if they are not captured no protests will have to be made. It is true that this would mean the loss of quite a lot of money through the suspension of trade, but it is argued that this loss would be less than the cost of a war maintained to protect our rights.

Far from being a method of preventing war, this accepts war; instead of discouraging war, it encourages it. With such a policy, the United States—the only people in the world to consider such an attitude—announces to all states which think of going to war that the United States will stand out of their way; and it assures such states that they may conduct the war in any fashion which pleases them, and that the United States will uncomplainingly endure any injuries which the belligerent, in its unlicensed conduct of the war, may care to inflict upon them. Under the Kellogg Pact, war was to be regarded as illegal; under the neutrality legislation, it is encouraged.

It is a humiliating and ignoble position for a great state. It surrenders completely to the god of war; it gives up all rights as a nation whenever war comes along, and all responsibility for maintaining law and peace in the world. Again the question must be asked: is there anything more important than peace? For the sole purpose of this legislation is to keep the United States out of war; it disavows any intent to stop war in general. It is difficult enough to explain refusal to share in the community task of maintaining community rights; it is even more difficult to explain refusal to stand up for one's own rights. It is an attitude inexplicably inconsistent with the character and temperament of the average American, who certainly believes in upholding his own rights, even to the extent of fighting for them, and who has often urged interference in the affairs of other states, in the name of justice or humanity.

The result of this particular kind of neutrality is, of course, the reign of the criminal in international society. One cannot get rid of crime by surrendering to it; it must be fought with every possible weapon. To surrender to war in this fashion means that the war-making state is left free to become more and more powerful until the day arrives when it feels able to attack even the mighty United States. Far from bringing security, it invites attack. Civilization has never reached its present stage of advancement through such supine surrender to crime; nor has the United States attained its present position of importance in the world by submissive dealings with those who would impose upon them.

In the reaction against war which followed upon the World War, many distorted explanations of war have gained hearing. The entry of the United States into that war has been variously explained as caused by business men greedy for war profits; by munitions makers seeking "blood money"; by bankers, for the protection of their loans; by propaganda; by the reckless political act of the President and other statesmen; etc. Each is put forward, and each gains currency for the moment, as the sole and complete explanation of the war. Of course, it cannot be so simply explained; but the result of such expositions has been to leave much confusion in the public mind as to the causes of war, and much skepticism as to the justification for maintaining rights. Why should we expend our money and our blood to protect a greedy trader or banker in a foreign country? Why should we struggle for the "freedom of the seas" to satisfy the selfish desires of a few war profiteers? Recent revelations, some of them scandalous, some of them sensationalized, have led many Americans to inquire whether they should support so-called rights which seem so much abused.

Of course, our problem cannot be so simply explained away; there are deeper and more fundamental issues at stake than the profits of the few who take advantage of war. The question is not whether the Standard Oil Company shall be deprived of its trade and profits; that is approaching the matter backwards. The true question is: Shall the entire community of nations be called upon to suffer simply because two states have run amok and gone to war with each other? Aside from exceptional war profits, which can be and should be restrained, must every state restrict its ordinary trade and activities and suffer a loss simply because other states resort to forbidden use of violence, instead of using the means of pacific settlement demanded by the community? Thomas Jefferson called attention to this in a letter to Livingston of September 9,

1801: "War between two nations cannot diminish the rights of the rest of the world remaining at peace. The doctrine that the rights of nations remaining quietly in the exercise of moral and social duties are to give way to the convenience of those who prefer plundering and murdering one another is a monstrous doctrine; and ought to yield to the more rational law, that 'the wrong which two nations endeavor to inflict on each other, must not infringe on the rights or conveniences of those remaining at peace.' . . . Shall two nations, turning tigers, break up in one instant the peaceable relations of the whole world?" Jefferson tried vainly, the United States being a weak state acting by itself, to support this view; it can only be maintained by joint action. Today, with neutrality in disrepute, and the community of nations organized, it is possible to make such a position effective.

We have already seen that we live in an interdependent community, in which trade and intercourse is a community necessity. Many states could not exist without such intercourse; even the United States would suffer without it. No doubt the trader is seeking his own gain; so is the baker and the groceryman in every hamlet of the world. But all are performing functions of importance to the community, and if they are not protected in it, the whole community suffers. It is no solution of the problem of war to say that individual traders are selfish, and must trade at their own risk. This is looking through the small end of the telescope: it is war which should be censured, and not the desire to continue the normal activities of life. It is the warmaker who should be penalized, and not the innocent bystander. There is no reason why the Standard Oil Company, or a "hot dog" salesman, or even a student desiring to study in Europe, should have to suffer inconvenience simply because Italy decides to invade Ethiopia.

If rights are to be maintained, it must be at a cost. This cost may be in terms of economic sacrifice, or in terms of military action. If it is the former, our own unaided stoppage of trade with the belligerents in accordance with the present neutrality legislation will do nothing to stop war—it is not intended to accomplish this; nor will it provide escape from danger for ourselves. If, however, all nations agreed to stop trade with a belligerent, the result might be to render him powerless to continue the war, which would mean reduction in our own economic loss. If we are to suffer such economic loss, let it not be in a cowardly and profitless attempt to escape risks for ourselves alone; if we are to suffer, let it be for a worthwhile end. Certainly our danger is less if we prevent war than if we merely try to escape its consequences after it has started. Moreover, the loss to ourselves would be less if the economic action is jointly assumed under an equitable arrangement by the entire community than with the complete suspension of our trade which would be necessary under the theory of escaping risks.

The same reasoning holds true for military action, if that should be required against a warmaker. If we wish to maintain our rights, we may do so through our own unaided military efforts or through the cooperation of the entire community of nations; the latter should certainly be cheaper, more efficient, and safer. It would mean, of course, that the community would decide what those rights are; if we are not willing to submit to such a decision, we need never hope to get rid of war. It would mean, too, helping other states in quarrels "which do not concern us" (they all concern us nowadays), but the total cost of participation in all such adventures would probably be less than the cost of one war fought by ourselves alone.

Neutrality, it has been said, is climbing a tree to escape a forest fire. It is an apt figure. You may say that a forest fire is a nasty thing, and that you will have nothing to do with it; but if you allow it to get going, it is fairly sure to have something to do with you. The safest procedure is to get out and fight it and stop it: and there is very little chance of your succeeding in this effort by yourself, or of the other fellow stopping it without your aid. You may suffer in fighting it; you may even lose your life; but you are even more apt to suffer disaster if you do not fight it. And war, in these days, spreads with the rapidity and destructiveness of a forest fire. The only way to stop war is to fight it.

It may be said that this discussion of neutrality is irrelevant to the purposes of this book. It is true that neutrality is not a method by which one can hope to eliminate war. It simply accepts war as a fact; it is a concomitant of war, and, like armaments, will disappear when war disappears. It has been argued that a strict observance of neutrality would restrain the spread of war —which is certainly no longer true; and that such observance of the law would hold the conduct of war within proper boundaries. But neutrality makes no effort to prevent war, nor does it offer any substitute for the functions which war is supposed to perform. It is a totally negative, or passive conception; it represents no more than a selfish desire to escape war after it starts. Nevertheless, it is of importance in our investigation because it brings to a head the most fundamental issue which faces the world in its efforts to stop war—the issue is between isolation and collective action, the issue between doing nothing and doing something. We turn now to the other side of the problem.

CHAPTER IX

THE LEAGUE OF NATIONS

The most famous of the methods by which it has been attempted to stop war is the League of Nations—though it should be remembered that this organization has other purposes as well. The Preamble to its Covenant begins with the words: "In order to promote international co-operation and to achieve international peace and security"; and much more of its energy is devoted to the former than to the latter purpose. Its usefulness has been so well established in the field of cooperation that, if its authority to deal with war should be taken away from it, it would doubtless continue to exist and to perform important functions. The United States itself, though not obligated to the League, participates in these non-political activities to an extent equalled by very few of the Members themselves of the League. And, of course, these activities do much to relieve the pressure of war.

Our interest, however, lies in the methods by which the League of Nations endeavors to control war. We stated at the outset of this study that it will be necessary, before war can be eliminated, to provide means for settling disputes, for remedying wrongs, and for enforcing rights. Of the various schemes under consideration, only the League of Nations makes a conscious effort to serve all these functions. It alone has machinery and organization; it alone offers any attempt at authority or coercion for these purposes; and what it has is inadequate.

The League of Nations is a representative body, composed of three organs: the Assembly, in which each state has an equal voice; the Council, in which the Great Powers formerly had control, but in which they now constitute only a small minority; and the Secretariat, whose members represent no state, but attempt to maintain an international character. It has no President, no executive head; it has no legislature with power to edict laws; it has no court with compulsory jurisdiction. The rudiments of a legislature are there; there is an excellent court, whose compulsory jurisdiction is steadily increasing; there is nothing which can be said really to have an executive character, though the Council performs some directive functions. The chief advance which it represents over the older system is an organized and centralized system of machinery through which states may act in agreement if they wish; its chief weakness is the lack of motive power to turn the wheels of this machinery.

For the performance of the first of the three functions mentioned above, the League of Nations has created an elaborate system for the peaceful settlement of disputes. Every dispute, of whatever nature, must be submitted either to arbitration or judicial settlement, if it is a legal question; otherwise, to inquiry by the Council. If the disputant states decide to arbitrate, the decision is final, and the matter is ended. No state can go to war before the end of a period of three months following the award; and all Members of the League are obligated not to go to war against the state which accepts the award. This means that all states are free to go to war against the state which refuses the award; it would have been more effective had all members been obligated to take up arms against the state which refused to accept the award.

Should the disputants decide not to arbitrate, then they must refer their quarrel to the Council. The effort of the Council is to find a compromise satisfactory to both; if it succeeds—i.e., if both accept—the affair is ended. If either or both refuse to accept the recommendations of the Council, and the Council is unanimous in its recommendation, the situation is the same as follows the award of an arbitral decree; that is, no state can go to war against the state which accepts the Council recommendation, but any state can go to war against the state which refuses it. But if the Council is unable to reach an unanimous accord (disputants excepted), then the situation is wide open, and any state may fight as it wishes.

The obligatory system for the settlement of disputes is thus fairly complete, though with one large gap, and some smaller ones, through which war remains legitimate. But, in addition to the provisions within the Covenant itself, there are many other treaties which impose duties of pacific settlement through agencies of the League of Nations. The Permanent Court of International Justice, while an autonomous institution, is part of the League system. Some forty states have now accepted the obligation, by signing the "Optional Clause," of submitting disputes of a legal nature to the Court for final settlement. The Council of the League may also ask the Court for an advisory opinion upon legal phases of questions referred to them. There are multilateral treaties, such as the "General Act of Geneva" to which states may accede in whole or in part; and there are innumerable bilateral treaties. Added up, these various treaties bind practically every state in the world—except the United States of America—to submit every dispute either to arbitration or to conciliation; and most of them make use of the League agencies for this purpose.

The chief difficulty with this wide range of obligations is that it is unsystematic. The Covenant of the League itself, as we saw, leaves some gaps; the various other obligations may overlap or conflict, or, on the other hand, may leave gaps between them. They need to be concentrated into a more uniform system of obligations, administered by the League; it is not fair that some states should escape obligations incumbent upon others, or that any state should remain its own judge. The field of compulsory jurisdiction needs to be extended, to apply equally to all states. And the system is further lacking in that cases submitted to the conciliatory process, where it is claimed that no legal question is at stake, may not receive a final and binding decision. Granted all this, the League is nevertheless well equipped for the pacific settlement of disputes; certainly, there is nothing else in the world which can compare with it.

This system offers ample opportunity for settling a dispute upon its merits. It is important, however, to distinguish between the merits of a dispute, and the methods by which the dispute is to be resolved. When a policeman finds two persons fighting on the street, he does not stop to inquire as to which has justice upon his side; the policeman's function is not to judge between the disputants, but to prevent the use of violence between them; he is to ensure that the dispute will be referred to proper agencies for decision upon its merits, and not to a decision by superior force. What can the League of Nations do in this respect?

If a Member of the League refuses to make use of the means of pacific adjustment, it is forbidden to resort to force. It may not make war against the state which accepts pacific settlement, though other states may make war against it, since it has not accepted this settlement. The obligation against force is reinforced by Article 10 of the Covenant, under which Members of the League undertake to respect and preserve, as against external aggression, the territorial integrity and existing political independence of Members. The principle herein stated is fundamental, the first rule to be applied by any government. Within the state it means that there must be no attack upon life or property; in terms of international law, it forbids the acquisition of title through conquest. Its importance is witnessed by the fact that, though the United States rejected it in 1919, she applied it, in the Hoover-Stimson doctrine, against Japan in 1931. The League has not, however, made much of this rule; it may safely be asserted that the use of force in international affairs will not be ended until this rule is made effective.

So far as protecting rights goes, the League thus declares illegitimate the use of force against those rights. What can it do when this prohibition is disregarded, and force is nevertheless illegally employed? By the terms of Article 16, a state which resorts to war in disregard of its covenants under Articles 12, 13, and 15, is deemed to have committed an act of war against all other Members of the League; the latter are thereupon obligated to undertake certain measures of coercion. These measures have come to be called "sanctions"; they correspond to the authority exercised by a state to enforce its laws. This is the first time that the society of nations has ever attempted to organize measures of coercion against the sovereign states which compose it; the effort must indubitably be attended not only with creaking of machinery, but also with hesitations upon the part of those who are supposed to operate it.

In the first place, such coercion can only be undertaken against a state which has gone to war, and has gone to war in disregard of Articles 12, 13, and 15—which contain the obligations for peaceful settlement above discussed. This, for example, leaves Article 10, the backbone of the system, without the support of sanctions; and other parts as well. Even the question of whether a state is at war is more difficult than might be thought. Next, who is to make the decision as to whether a state has illegally resorted to war? According to present interpretation, each Member decides this important question for itself; there is no central authority to which the power of decision has been delegated, and whose decision binds all Members. As a result of this peculiar situation, there may be hesitation and uncertainty in the application of sanctions; if consultation does not bring agreement as to which is the "aggressor" state, sanctions cannot be applied. In principle—weak as this might be in practice—a member state must proceed to the application of economic sanctions as soon as it has decided that a certain state has gone to war illegally.

Sanctions, under the Covenant, may be of two kinds: economic and military. The former are obligatory upon Members; the latter are entirely voluntary. If sufficient agreement has been reached as to which is the state against which sanctions should be applied, the states so agreeing are expected to break off all economic and financial relations with that state. Of course, in such a situation, it is conceivable that some states would be acting against one belligerent and some against the other; a sort of economic civil war in the community of nations. An agency authorized to decide for all is needed. Once the obligation is operative, states are confronted with the difficulty that no system for this procedure has been established; there is no economic general staff. Its first application, in the Italo-Ethiopian affair, revealed many difficulties, some of which had long been anticipated. It has always been obvious that some states would suffer more than others, in each particular case, by suspending intercourse with the delinquent state; but no system has been established for the equalization of these burdens. The same situation appears with regard to individuals within each state; the oil or steel industries, perhaps, would lose more than the butter and egg industries. To overcome such difficulties would require much study and effective supervision from above; but this has not yet been done. Again, adjacent states may be in danger of military attack from the aggressor state if it applies economic sanctions; this was Mussolini's threat if an oil embargo was instituted. For such states the League offers no protection; it has not the authority to order military action in any case.

In spite of these difficulties, the first effort to apply economic sanctions went forward surprisingly well. All but two or three states were able to agree that Italy was the offender; practically all were able to agree upon the measures to be taken. The insurmountable difficulties came from outside the League. Economic sanctions cannot be properly effective unless they are universally applied. If one or more states with large resources are willing to trade with the state under coercion, it is futile for other states to break off their trade. The absence of the United States alone, or the uncertainty concerning her course of action, has made it almost impossible for the League to go further than the United States has done. It was unable to set an embargo upon arms until the United States did; it was unable to embargo oil and other commodities because the United States did not. It would, of course, be a vain gesture for Members of the League to cut off their trade with Italy, when that state might obtain all that it needed from the United States. Their sole purpose in making such a sacrifice would be to make it impossible, or difficult, for the aggressor state to carry on the war; in result, they would not succeed if the United States should sell to Italy, and they would have accomplished no more than to lose their markets in Italy to the United States.

The difficulty goes even further; it becomes danger. Members of the League, under Article 16, are expected not only to prevent trade from their own territories, but also to stop such trade between the aggressor state and any other state, whether Member of the League or not. This is the correct principle; but as a practical measure, it would be absurd to try it, when such a powerful state as the United States would be the one to be coerced. The result, it was feared—since the United States had fought more than one war to uphold her neutral rights—would be to cause a war greater than the one they were trying to stop. This situation has long been known; efforts to strengthen the sanctions of the League, such as the Geneva Protocol, have more than once foundered on the rock of Britain's unwillingness to risk such a conflict with the United States.

Considering these difficulties and weaknesses, it is surprising that economic sanctions have been carried as far and as successfully as they have in their first trial. It is nevertheless clear that they cannot have the effect needed without the cooperation of non-members, particularly the United States. Military sanctions, on the other hand, are not required under the Covenant, though one may think of a moral obligation to contribute to military sanctions when the Council so recommends. We have already suggested that economic measures may be resisted by military attack, and that in such a case the victim of the attack could well expect support from his fellows. It has been argued, in general, that military measures may be simpler and more efficient, and as cheap and merciful, as economic sanctions.

From the viewpoint of enforcing rights, then, the League does not have adequate power; its more powerful members, if not all of them, do not feel confident that their rights will be protected at present as well as they might protect them by their own efforts. It needs to be strengthened in its constitutional law, and by the adherence or cooperation of non-members. On the other hand, it is the only method which even attempts to substitute for war as a means of preserving rights, and it has gone a long way in that direction.

Finally, does the League supply a method of remedying wrongs? Never in the history of the nations has any provision for this important function been made; and its lack has often led to war, since no other recourse existed. International law had the fundamental rule that treaties must be obeyed; but it had no means of changing a treaty which was unjust without the consent of those who profited from it. Yet, it is not the function of law to change situations; this is a legislative function, and the community of nations had no legislature. It may again be said that the League of Nations has gone further in this direction than ever in history, and further than is proposed by any other method for controlling war; but it must also be said that this is the most inadequate part of the League system. In the past, conferences and voluntary agreement have been the only means of changing unjust situations; the League has improved this method by regularizing and improving conferences, by calling all nations to attend them, and by attracting the widest attention to their efforts. Further, the Council may inquire into disputes, and make recommendations as to changes in legal situations necessary to reach a just settlement of the dispute. And Article 19 of the Covenant is the first wedge driven into the legal *status quo;* the wedge seems indeed to have become stuck, but the first blow was driven. This article provides no more than that the Assembly may recommend the reconsideration (by signatories) of treaties which have become inapplicable. It is an advance, in that it is thus admitted that such treaties are the legitimate concern of states other than the signatories; and in that public opinion may be focused upon the state which refuses to reconsider an inequitable situation. But as a means of aiding the "havenots" against the "haves," or of compelling a victor to revise a treaty obtained by force, it is wholly inadequate. It has been further weakened, during the early years of the League, by the efforts of the victors in the World War to prevent its use; efforts which were the more successful since it is the duty of the League to uphold existing international law, and since states which might have resisted such efforts were not in the League.

To sum up, the League of Nations makes a conscious effort to provide for the functions which must be performed in international society before war can be abolished. It has a very good system for settling disputes peaceably, with a few gaps needing to be filled. It has machinery for common enforcement of rights far stronger than any yet devised, though still not so strong as to convince states that they may disarm, or that they may turn their interests entirely over to the League for protection. And it makes the first attempt, inadequate as it is, to provide what the society of nations most needs, a means of changing unjust situations without the consent of all the parties concerned.

It is to be observed, too, that the program of the League embraces all the proposals, of a positive character, which have been discussed in the preceding chapters. It rests upon the principle of collective security, and therefore rejects neutrality in principle; likewise, it makes no use of the negative concept of passive resistance. It does make provision for the reduction of armaments, and has conducted a most intense campaign in that direction—only to conclude that security must precede disarmament. It has studied the private trade in arms, and long ago concluded a treaty on that subject, which has recently been ratified by the United States. As a method of education for peace, nothing can equal it: it commands newspaper space; it has its own radio facilities; it reaches into the curricula of the schools of every nation; it affords the widest forum for public discussion that the world has ever known. It studies continuously the causes of war, and through research and conference and agreement is steadily, if slowly, removing many of those causes. While it does not formally declare war illegal, it does much more effectively than the Pact of Paris make war illegal, for it establishes definite obligations, and has machinery for putting them into effect.

It is unfortunate that so important an effort should have fallen prey to political controversy; and it is well to recommend the use of common sense in discussing it, for, whether right or wrong, it is an issue of vast significance to the world. It is clear—by way of illustration of the need for common sense—that no Member of the League can be compelled to go to war, or to use its armed force, unless it so desires; on the other hand, it is clear that the League cannot hope to succeed unless its members are willing to employ force, when necessary, to achieve its ends. Again, if it is to be criticised on the ground that it does not sufficiently care for the "have-nots" as against the "haves," it is well to recall that within each state there are many havenots who are dissatisfied, among individuals; it is not suggested, however, that domestic government be abandoned because of its inability to solve this difficult question. The charge is made that certain states are using and always will use the League of Nations to accomplish their own selfish purposes, which is undoubtedly true, as it is true in any human society; but it is not to be expected that citizens can rid themselves of a Tammany Hall by refusing to vote, or that they can assist the League to conduct itself properly by abstaining from participation in its work. Similarly, it is said that the League was too weak to stop Japan and Italy; it seems reasonable to conclude therefrom that the League should be strengthened rather than that it should be forsaken.

A dispassionate observer of the League could well conclude that it has had more successes than failures, and that it has shown potentialities as an instrument for the control of war, though it is inadequate and defective in many respects. Upon the basis of the criteria which we have been using throughout this book, it may be said that the League not only proceeds in the right direction, but that it embraces all the proposals for dealing with war which meet these criteria, and provides machinery for putting them to use. It seems safe to say that the only alternative to the League of Nations as a means of controlling war is a better League of Nations. There is no alternative to collective action.

CHAPTER X

CONCLUSIONS

The purpose of this inquiry, it will be recalled, was to discover a means of controlling war; and the foregoing discussions should establish—if it needed to be established—that war cannot be handled in the simple fashion which some are content to try. It is not enough just to hate war; there is enough opposition to war now if it could be directed into the proper channel. Nor is it enough simply to disregard war, as others seem to wish. The necessary objective is, not merely to escape war, but to stop it; for when war starts, there is no telling who will be seriously hurt by it. On the other hand, it is probably as incorrect to say that war can be completely eradicated, as that all crime, or all use of force, between individuals can be eradicated. The extent to which it can be controlled will be measured by the intelligence and ingenuity of mankind and the willingness of peoples to take the steps necessary.

Not all the proposals for the abolition of war have been here discussed. Many fantastic proposals have been made, from requiring soldiers to wear derby hats on parade, to hating one's cat instead of one's enemy, or putting statesmen, or bankers, or munitions manufacturers, or someone, in the front ranks of battle. Some of these suggestions might be regarded as intelligent if the assumption were correct that war results from the innate desire, of human beings to fight—always, of course human beings whose nature is quite different from that of the speaker! But this is a false assumption: the reason for war is deeper and more fundamental than a mere combative instinct. Force has always been called upon because it is the ultimate method by which peoples, whether individually or in national groups, have been able to achieve their desires. It is not war which is desired, but other things, good or bad, which it is hoped can be attained through the use of war. It is logical to believe that, if a more effective method could be discovered for accomplishing these ends, that method would be employed rather than war.

Most of the proposals which we have discussed contribute something to the problem of finding a substitute for war; but in each case, something more was needed. Thus disarmament might make national wars cheaper and less bloody, but since it cannot aid in the satisfaction of national desires, it is not successful; since it does not offer security, it is not accepted. The same is true of the effort to control the trade in arms; and in either case, the objective could not be attained without international supervision. Education is important toward building support for whatever method, but it must be an international rather than a national education, and this implies international direction. It is highly important to remove the causes of war, but this cannot be done by wishing them away; it would require continuing international machinery with authority to make decisions and to enforce them. There may be potentialities in passive resistance, as yet unknown; but if it is a weapon, it can be used and abused just as war is, unless it is brought under the same control as is now sought for war. To outlaw war on paper has been shown by recent events—as well as by history—to be a futile gesture; it can mean something only if backed by a force superior to that of any state which might seek to break that law. And the League of Nations, which includes most of the above suggestions in its program, has not been able to prevent war in recent tests.

What, then, can be done? Let us summarize and analyze.

There can be no doubt that there are some principles, some ideals, which we as human beings wish to maintain, and for which we are willing to sacrifice much, even life. Even the absolute pacifist is willing to sacrifice his life for what he believes to be right. There are many who believe that war as a method of upholding such ideals is stupid and sinful, and who refuse to participate in it; they nevertheless have some principles in which they firmly believe, and for which they would be willing to sacrifice much. It is this conviction, upon which civilization is builded—that there are some principles which must be maintained—which is our necessary starting point.

In each of these schemes, we have been forced back against the need for international organization, in some form; no other solution appears possible except ideal anarchy, a stage to which we have not yet arrived. Nations more and more depend upon each other, and continuously demands are being made for limitations upon the freedom of states to do as they wish. For national sovereignty, in the society of nations, corresponds to individual liberty within the state; and it will inevitably be limited as the community of nations feels necessary. Here is the ancient dilemma of man, which has led him to create government; it involves the ancient and fundamental problem of government: how far may individual liberty go? The answer to that question varies with circumstances; but always it has been an answer furnished by the community as a whole, and not an answer furnished by an individual member thereof. The boundary line of that liberty, whether of individuals or of nations, has been steadily decreasing, and this not because of an outside coercion; it results from an internal pressure. The most powerful states ask for new international law and submit to that law, because it is to their interest to do so. So powerful a state as France must submit to the majority in the Postal Union, because postal communications are essential to her; recently, the community of nations has gone further than ever before in joint pressure against Italy, because Italy had gone beyond the limits of her freedom of action as agreed upon in the community.

That is one side of the picture; it must also be looked at from the viewpoint of the individual state. States are faced with the choice between continuous fighting, in support of their right to do as they please, and submission to community agreement. A state may choose between continuous fighting in support of any and all of its ambitions, or collective action in support of some of them. If it is a small state, there can be little doubt as to its choice, for only by combination with others can it hope to protect any of its rights. The large state, confident in its own strength, will then be faced by a combination which will be too strong for it; and the combination will have no sympathy for that state, since it is unwilling to cooperate with others. The more powerful the state, the more powerful will be the combination of others against it; this is assured by the desire of other states to exist and to have some rights. The road of history is strewn with the wrecks of states which have sought to have their own way, and that long before the pressure of modern interdependence began to be felt. Every state, then, stands to gain in the protection of those rights which the community agrees upon; it stands to lose in the maintenance of those demands which go beyond what the community thinks is right. And since it stands to lose the latter in any case—as the record of history shows—the balance stands in favor of joining in with the community for the maintenance of rights agreed upon by all.

As to this choice, the lesson of history is clear and unequivocal. Eternal struggle is exhausting; the reason of man has led him always to surrender some of his individual liberty in order to secure more effective protection for the most of that liberty. He has found it a risky business to maintain that liberty by his own strength, for its assertion leads to conflicts and to combinations against him, even if he does not run into someone more powerful than he, and lose everything. Humanity has found that the effort necessary to protect fundamental rights amounts to much less when divided between the members of the community, with a common organization and authority to administer it. Historically, too, no individual has been permitted to stand outside the community and to follow his own desires; he has been compelled, by physical force, if necessary, to submit to the community law.

This is the inevitable course of development in the society of nations. It has been going on at a rapid rate during the past half century or more, and it has accelerated with such speed that the historian will be able to record no period of political development so rapid as that during the past fifteen or twenty years—all of it in the direction of community law and control, and away from unrestrained national sovereignty. States find it impossible to endure the cost of non-participation in these developing activities; thus, the United States has come to take a greater share in the non-political activities of the League than do most of its members, in spite of its desire for isolation.

We arrive, then, at the conclusion that states must share in community action, and may have only such rights as are agreed upon in the community. Yet this development has not gone so far as to induce states to surrender their arms and give up the right to make war. This cannot be hoped for until states can have a sense of security for themselves. Now, insecurity derives from the fear of force; and force can be combated, in the long run, only by force. This, too, is an accepted lesson of history; but the community of nations has not yet decided whether each state shall exercise this force for itself, or whether that force shall be made a monopoly of the community, to be used only under the authority of the community, as is done within the state. The decision of this question is the most important issue which now faces the community of nations. It is clear, on the one hand, that the community of nations will not protect the rights of an individual member as determined by that member; if it determines its own rights, it must maintain its own rights, and that by war. On the other hand, a state will not be prepared to surrender its own judgment and its own protection, and to accept the rights agreed upon for it by the community of nations, unless it can be assured in return of protection by the community; and this means by physical force.

We thus arrive at our final conclusion: that states must surrender some of their national sovereignty and accept such rights as are agreed upon by the community; that for this purpose an international organization is necessary; and that this international organization must be backed by an overwhelming physical force, strong enough to assure to each state the security which it seeks. Until such an international government is created, it is not to be expected that any state will surrender its right to make war; not until it can be assured that its disputes can be settled, its wrongs can be remedied, and its rights enforced. Reluctant as one may be to arrive at this conclusion, it cannot be denied that physical force is essential in such a system. If any state uses force, other states, or the community, must be ready to reply with force; there is no other answer. The economic sanctions of the League of Nations were impotent against the threat of force made by Mussolini; the only answer to this threat was to use force against him, and the Members of the League were not prepared to go so far. It is no reply to this situation to say that it replaces war with war. When organized government uses force against a lawbreaker, it is not war, but police action, wholly justifiable. And even if one calls it war, it would nevertheless be essential. The community of nations has recently gone as far as is possible without the use of force; its failure is conclusive proof that it must be prepared to back its decisions, against a state which resorts to arms, with force.

The issue faces the United States squarely today, and is indeed peculiarly addressed to her. Most of the rest of the world have accepted the idea of collective action. Consequently, the United States is reproached with obstructing, and of having caused the failure of, the efforts of the community to achieve law and order between nations; on the other hand, she is faced with the dangers inherent in a situation in which she stands alone—danger of discrimination and reprisals, and ultimately of conflict. No community, organized for the maintenance of law and order, can allow one of its members freedom of action.

There is no doubt that any people, the American people included, will endeavor to maintain what they conceive to be their rights. At the present moment, this does not appear to be true of the United States, where passive resistance and surrender of neutral rights are loudly urged. It is safe to regard this as a temporary aberration, due to the great confusion of arguments in this country as to the proper foreign policy to be followed. At the beginning of our history we were a weak nation, fearful of other states and bound by no ties to them; on the contrary, divinely separated from them by thousands of miles of water. We were so completely occupied with the development of our own resources that we had no time to think of other nations. Isolation was then a fact, and it naturally affected our foreign policy and our public opinion. It is no longer a fact, but it is not surprising that traditions which grew up during this early period should still affect our thinking. During the twentieth century we were beginning to realize that we had become a part of the world; but we were thrown into a state of confusion from which we have not yet recovered by the bitter debates over the League of Nations in 1919. More recently, the fear of war has stirred up other divagations. Books have been written to prove that one thing only—a different thing in each book—was responsible for the World War; and sections of public opinion branched off on the trail of each of these evils, in the belief that by repairing it, war could be stopped. Various pacifist groups, each sincerely believing that it had found the answer, put forth such conflicting views that the average citizen did not know whom to follow. The confusion in our thinking is amazing, and resulted in the neutrality legislation, based upon the theory, though without fully realizing it, that the American people should surrender all their rights to war-making states.

This, however, is so thoroughly out of step with American character and traditions that one may be sure it is temporary. The American people have always stood up for their own rights, and even for the rights of others. They have expressly reserved, even in the present confusion, the right of self-defense, construed in the widest terms; and the right to fight for the Monroe Doctrine. There is no doubt that for other causes, too, they would spring to arms, in the absence of other means for protecting rights which they might regard as important. And if this be true, the question which they must answer is: shall the United States fight alone to maintain those rights, or with the aid of other members of the community?

The confusion of thought above mentioned is further exemplified in the inconsistent attitude of the people of the United States toward the League of Nations today. We rejected the League (in part) because we were opposed to sanctions. Yet recently the American has been rushing down for the morning paper to find out how the League was getting along in its fight with Italy. When the League voted sanctions, or when its Members applied sanctions, we were wildly enthusiastic—although the League was doing just what we say it should not do! And when we heard that the League was hesitating to apply sanctions, or was not moving fast enough, then we berated the League and asserted that we would have nothing to do with such an institution—because it was failing to do the very things we think it should not do! All of which goes to show that the American's heart is in the right place, even if he does not know it. The American people are not content to sit back and let war rule the world; they are not content to allow injustice to be done, even in foreign lands. They never have been; our history records many cases in which we have ardently upheld the rights of others, even to the extent of war. We have never withdrawn into hermit-like seclusion, not even today. For the very Senators who, on one day, vote against joining the World Court because it is connected with the busybody League of Nations, on the next day introduce resolutions calling for an investigation of the treatment of Catholics in Mexico, or of the action of Japan in Manchuria!

Likewise, the American people do not object to sanctions. They have never hesitated to use force to maintain their own rights; and the enthusiasm with which they have greeted the application of sanctions against Italy shows that they have no objection to the use of sanctions against a war-making state. Practically everything which the League of Nations does, whether in the field of international cooperation, or in the field of the maintenance of peace, finds support in America. There is no doubt that most Americans approve of the efforts of the League in practically all fields; what they object to is participation in such efforts. They are willing to go it alone for the same ends; they are willing to applaud other states working for those ends; but they refuse any joint commitments.

They are now more than ever disappointed in the League of Nations; but if one may judge by various expressions of public opinion in recent years, they more than ever believe in the principles and purposes of the League. Their criticisms are addressed rather to the selfish purposes of Members of the League, and to what they regard as the misuse of the League. Perhaps, if the present League were scrapped, they would be willing to accept another organization to support the principles in which they believe, and in which the League believes. This, however, is a remote possibility. The League of Nations is an established institution, supported by most of the states of the world; it cannot be expected that they would scrap their own building and build anew merely to suit a whim of the United States. They would doubtless, however, be willing to accept changes and modifications. Indeed, after fifteen years of testing, they are of their own accord ready to make changes which might result in improvement. If the United States would indicate the changes which she desires made before she would enter the League, there is little doubt that important revisions of the Covenant would be made to meet her desires.

Very probably, the American people would be unwilling at present to commit this nation to the use of force in support of the decisions of the League. This is unfortunate; it is unfortunate also that other nations are unwilling to go so far. No such obligation, of course, is now found in the Covenant of the League; but it would be desirable to have the United States in the League even if it were necessary to revise the Covenant to make sure that no such use of force could be obligatory. Her entry would not only regularize the vast amount of non-political cooperation with the League which we now have (with no share in the overhead cost) but would encourage and aid at least in the settlement of disputes and in the remedying of wrongs. It is not enough to say that we can be counted upon to do the right thing; upon such a foundation of unsupported promise, the community of nations cannot build with confidence. In business, in religion, in sports, and in general, the American has learned the value of cooperation, and has builded accordingly; if we as a nation have no selfish motives which would have to be supported by our own strength, we need no more hesitate at international cooperation. Politically, the United States set the world the example of combining jealous and separatist nations under a common system of government, and it has been remarkably successful.

But, whatever the United States may willingly consent to do, it is inevitable that the present development in the community of nations should continue and grow. Failures will lead to renewed efforts, as they always do when the need is important. The plague of fire has been much mitigated by improved methods of building, by stringent rules for fire prevention, and by centralized machinery for fighting fire. The science of aviation has developed to its present stage of usefulness after tragic failures, but these failures did not stop advance; on the contrary, they revealed defects and stimulated improvement. The present international organization is inadequate for preventing war, but when one looks back over the short span of years in which international relations have been revolutionized, and considers the opportunity for as rapid development during the coming years, he may well afford to be optimistic. International government will be given more authority as the need for it is realized; just as the United States of America, reluctantly organized under the Articles of Confederation, realized that a stronger system was needed, and set up the present Constitution. The pressure of circumstances is relentless.

This development is inevitable, in the light of political experience and of common sense; it is inevitable, too, that it must be backed by force. This force would be entirely different in character from war, which is the use of force by a state for its own purposes. The sanctions of physical force employed by the community of nations would be to prevent the selfish national use of force, and to uphold the law of the community. It corresponds to the use of force by the policeman within the state. But whatever one calls it, whether war or police, there must always be in the background a strength superior to that of any dissident.

It might happen that a combination of states would be formed strong enough to resist this force; it is the more probable in the early days of such a system, before the habit of obedience and cooperation is established. Again it must be said that perfection cannot be expected. It is to be hoped that such a situation would be as exceptional as the civil war within a state to which it corresponds; certainly, no one ever thinks of throwing domestic government overboard because of the possibility of civil war within the state. There are other complaints and fears. Doubtless it is true that France or England—or any other state—will attempt to manipulate the organization to advance its own ends; this is usually true in any political system; we try it at every conference the United States attends. But staying outside does nothing to stop such efforts; the result may simply be that states opposed to our interests may build up their strength, through our abstention, until they become dangerous to us. One does not combat Tammany Hall by refusing to vote; nor does the fact that Mr. Farley, or someone else, has more political power than the average person, incline us to discard our governmental system. Nor, again, does the fact that criminals object to having their individual liberty interfered with by the policeman's stick or gun incline us to deprive the policeman of his right to use force. Many such criticisms could be noted; all and more are found in the early history of any state.

It is important to say, however, that forcible sanctions are not enough, and international government must provide more than this. For, after all, the use of force, whether as war by a nation, or as sanctions by the community of nations, is only a means toward an end. The end is to secure justice, in its widest sense, for the greatest number. If force is employed, in either sense, to maintain an unjust *status quo,* it will inevitably be met by force. Some states are far better equipped with natural resources than others; the latter will not submit to starvation. Nor will existing laws and treaties be allowed to continue an unjust situation, simply because they are law and are backed by sanctions.

The situation is well portrayed in an excellent book by Simonds and Emeny, *The Price of Peace,* which, whether intentionally or not, is a strong argument for collective action backed by force. They point out what is undoubtedly now the chief weakness of the existing system: "The League of Nations constitutes an instrument uniquely designed to prevent war and without effective resource to remove those inequalities which great people will not endure peacefully." In any system, there must always be provided means for change and progress; sanctions used to maintain an existing status, with no means of change, will lead only to a more violent explosion in the long run. In this respect, the League is defective—though it offers much more in this direction than was possible before it was created. It needs the authority to change a legal situation without the consent of those states which profit from that situation; and its authority must again be backed by force. The "haves" will not divide up with the "havenots" until they are forced to it.

If the above conclusions are correct, it is obvious that we must have a much wider and stronger system of government between nations than we yet have. To quote Simonds and Emeny again: "Either the League constituted a substitute for war as a means of providing mankind with those things for which it has been fighting for untold thousands of years—justice, equality, and prosperity—or it did not." This is correct; it states the principle with which this book started; but the conclusion to be drawn from it is that the League must be strengthened. The League has gone further in this direction than any other human effort; it needs not to be scrapped, with the loss of all thus far gained, but to be improved. If its principles are sound—and they make possible the overwhelming power which Simonds and Emeny think is needed—then it should be used; if its machinery is inadequate, then it should be strengthened and improved. No other solution is offered. The only alternative is to fall back upon the old system; but that system necessitates the war which we are trying to eliminate.

The only proposal which attempts to offer a substitute for war as a means of settling disputes, remedying wrongs, and enforcing rights is the League of Nations. It is not satisfactory as it now stands; but, whether it stands or whether it be replaced by some other organization, the principles upon which it is founded and the objectives toward which it aims are correct. Since it is an accepted and established institution, it seems more logical to build upon it; to rebuild entirely would be wasted effort. Whether this particular institution survives or not is unimportant; but the system of collective security which it attempts to build is the only answer to the problem of war. There is no panacea; war must be attacked from all angles. To do this requires an international organization to which all states belong, willingly or not, with a program wide enough to meet all the needs for which war might be urged, and with a force behind it capable of overcoming all resistance.

Date Due
MAY 20